Lake District

William Forrester

photography by

Barry Stacey

HarperCollins*Publishers*

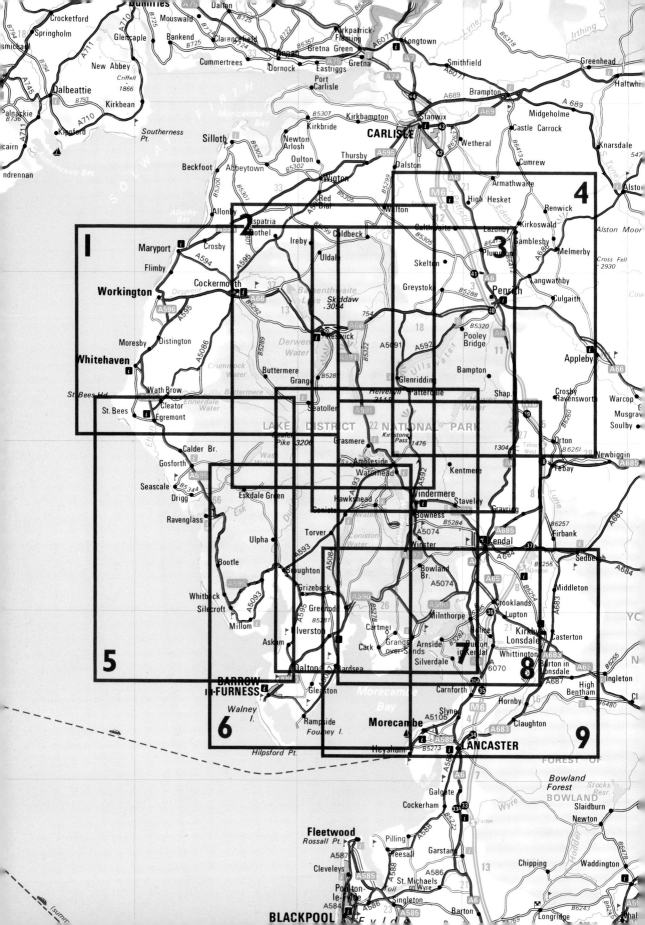

Contents

The North-West

Carling Knott, Loweswater

St Begas's church, Bassenthwaite

Preceding page: Borrowdale, looking from Seatoller towards Green Comb

There is a lot of variety in this small area – to the east are craggy mountains and well-loved lakes, and to the west a gently undulating plain stretching to a coastline teeming with docks and industry. And yet even amid this comparative ugliness, you'll find plenty of charming surprises, such as the isolated and ancient town of St Bees.

You can't really understand the North-West or the Lake District as a whole unless you look at its geology. The oldest rocks, at 500 million years, are found around Bassenthwaite. Called Skiddaw slates, they are not the type to roof your house with, because they break too easily. This slate wears away quickly too, so the mountains here have fine, smooth profiles. The mountains south of Buttermere are altogether different and made of harder, craggier volcanic rock laid down about 450 million years ago. To the west and under Workington, Maryport and Whitehaven are 300 million-year-old coal measures. St Bees is different again, with great red sandstone cliffs formed some 230 million years ago.

Industry isn't something one usually associates with the Lakes and yet this region used to be a major industrial area. Whitehaven, for example, was once the second largest port in the country after London. The town owes much of its rich

Maryport

Winter storm, Bassenthwaite Lake

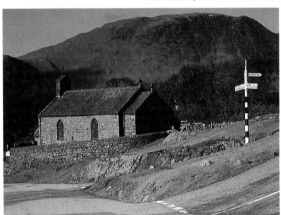

St John's church, Buttermere

history to its industrial past and has much to offer the visitor. By the mid 19th century, 200,000 tons of coal were being produced here annually and the pits eventually extended for 3 miles (5 km) under the sea. Other industries gradually sprang up, using both local and imported materials to produce detergent, sulphuric acid, cement and, of course, iron. The iron went to make cannons and ships. The wealth generated by all this trade and industry led to the importation of luxury items such as tobacco, spices, rum and sugar from the West Indies. It is hardly surprising that many of the local recipes seem very rich. A classic example is Cumberland Butter. This used to be a traditional

gift for a newborn baby: the Demerara sugar represented sweetness, the nutmeg and cinnamon zest, the butter a smooth path through life and the rum, of course, spirit!

Naturally, such prosperity was acquired at a cost to both people and the natural landscape. Coal-mining has always been a disfiguring and potentially dangerous business – Whitehaven, for example, lost 136 men and boys in a pit explosion in 1910 and a further 104 in 1947. Anyone with a feel for history will find plenty hereabouts to interest them.

Other signs of old industry can be found inland. The disused workings of the Buttermere and

Workington Castle

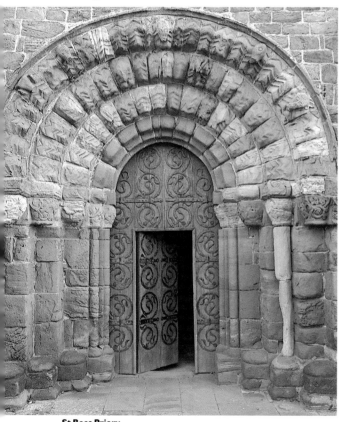

St Bees Priory

Buttermere

Westmorland Green Slate Company can still be seen at Honister Pass. The road from the west winds up beside the old tramway which moved slate mined from underground quarries called 'close heads'. Black powder was used to blast down to a depth of some 700 feet (225 m); gelignite would have shattered the slate totally. Large blocks of the green slate were brought up to be cut by diamond-tipped saws and then split and shaped in time-honoured fashion by hand. Only 10 per cent of the mined rock could be used. The rest was abandoned on 'spoil heaps', making a mess of the countryside.

Forestry is another controversial industry that has had an impact on the area. After World War I the new Forestry Commission decided that the bare hillsides in the Lake District could be made

St Bees Head

productive. The result was heavy-handed planting of conifers around Ennerdale Water and instant outrage among those who value Lakeland for its open views. The Commission has changed its views over the years and in the last decade the 13 miles (20 km) of Sitka spruce planted at Ennerdale have been mellowed by the addition of larch and broad-leaved trees.

This area of Lakeland is teeming with wildlife. At Bassenthwaite, a wildlife site of special scientific interest, you'll see rare plants and birdlife, and a fish (the vendace) so rare in England that the only other place you'll find it is in Derwentwater next door. A little farther on, at St Bees, is the only place in England where the black guillemot breeds.

The scenery is superb too. Buttermere wowed many early visitors to the Lakes and remains a

Whitehaven harbour

Honister Pass, looking towards High Stile

firm favourite. Fortunately, vehicles these days aren't defeated by the steepness of Honister Pass and you won't, as they used to, have to get out of your vehicle at this point and walk. The Lakes were toured for their views and yet most of these early visitors didn't want to see them as they really were. They'd turn their backs and gaze at the scenery through their hand-held Claude glasses, which tinted and framed every scene. Natural beauty was not appreciated for its own sake in those days but had to be brought up to certain aesthetic standards and 'improved upon'. Looking

at the views is still the most common visitor activity in the Lakes, but nowadays without the Claude glasses.

The Lake District has such a sorry reputation weather-wise that you've probably been wondering whether you'll see the scenery at all. Seathwaite has the dubious distinction of being this country's wettest inhabited spot, with an annual rainfall of 130 inches (325 cm). This doesn't mean that it is always raining here, just that you get a lot of rain at one go; 6 inches (15 cm) a day is not uncommon. The rainfall is exceptional because of

Wordsworth memorial, Cockermouth

Cockermouth

Above Crummock Water

Footpath, Crummock Water

Seathwaite's situation. The rainclouds are forced to rise by the mountains and, as a result, deposit their contents on the village below. The mountain tops excepted, which have a very harsh climate for most of the year, the rainfall in other parts of the region is about average for the country as a whole. The weather really does vary a great deal within a short distance. Grange, for example, is just a few miles from Seathwaite and has a dry, mild climate similar to that in Torquay. If it's raining in your valley or dale, take the advice of the locals and try another one!

11

❶ BUTTERMERE

The walk around the lake gives superb views. One of the great scandals of the 19th century involved Mary Robinson, the Beauty of Buttermere. She thought she'd married the Earl of Hopetoun's brother, only to discover that her husband was a bankrupt imposter. He was hanged and she later married a local farmer.

❷ COCKERMOUTH

This small, ancient market town is William Wordsworth's birthplace, and lies at the confluence of the rivers Derwent and Cocker. Wordsworth House (Main Street), the Georgian mansion where the poet spent his childhood, has been faithfully restored by the National Trust. The garden is especially lovely. (Open Apr–Nov weekdays; some Sats Apr–Sept) The Castlegate House Gallery (Castlegate Drive), built in 1739, contains Georgian sculpture, paintings and glass. (Open Mar– Dec, Mon–Wed and Fri–Sat) Those who like a bit more action will find it at the Cumberland Toy and Model Museum (Market Place), a fine collection of mainly British toys of the last 100 years. Among the many working toys is a large, vintage Hornby layout. Special exhibitions are held each year. (Open Feb–Nov daily ☕) At Jennings' Brewery (Brewery Lane) you can see local ale being produced. (Open daily, tours Apr–Oct) ☎ 01900 822634

For something completely different, go to Wythop Mill, Embleton (4 miles/7 km along the Bassenthwaite road). Here you'll see the old sawmill's overshot wheel and an exhibition of old woodworking machines. Coffee shop. (Open Apr–Oct, Tues–Sun. Phone 017687 76394)

❸ CRUMMOCK WATER

This lake is fed by two of the local sights – Scale Force and Loweswater. Scale Force is just to the west of the lake. Plummeting 172 feet (52 m), it is the highest waterfall in a district famous for them. To reach it, take the rough footpath from Buttermere. Far less strenuous are the walks at Holme Wood, on the west side of Loweswater.

❹ DALEHEAD BASE

Displays, craft days and guided walks are run here by the National Park. Refreshments are available. (Open Apr–Sept daily. Phone 017687 77294) You can reach Honister Pass (1176 ft/359 m) from the base and nearby there is a side road which branches off to the tiny hamlet of Seathwaite. From here you can walk to Stockley Bridge and the 140 foot (43 m) cascade of Taylor Gill Force.

❺ ENNERDALE WATER

A wild, remote and peaceful spot. Take the forest trail from the car park and viewpoint at Bowness Knott (north side of the lake).

❻ MARYPORT

The docks which once played a major role in this town's prosperity are now being restored as a boat haven. One of the attractions is the *Flying Buzzard*, a 1951 Clyde tugboat. (Open Easter–Oct daily. Phone 01900 815954 ♿ ☕) The Maritime Museum (Senhouse Street) tells the story of local boatbuilding and of two local lads: Fletcher Christian (of *Mutiny on the Bounty* fame) and Thomas Ismay (founder of the famous White Star shipping line). (Open Easter–Oct, Mon–Sat, Sun afternoons only) ☎ 01900 813738

❼ MIREHOUSE

This 17th-century house east of Bassenthwaite Lake has a fine collection of furniture, paintings and literary items. In the grounds you'll find the Norman church of St Bega, the Old Sawmill Tearoom and four adventure playgrounds! The grounds lead down to Bassenthwaite Lake, according to Tennyson the final resting place of King Arthur's sword, Excalibur. (Open Apr–Oct: grounds daily, house Sun, Wed, and Fri in Aug, afternoons only ☕. Phone 017687 72287)

❽ ST BEES

This village manages to combine scenic beauty and history. The church here used to be part of an ancient priory (founded c. AD 650). Don't miss the superb Norman door (1160) at the west end. The public school nearby dates back to 1583. You can reach the lighthouse by walking north from the car park and up the sandstone cliffs of St Bees Head (462 ft/90 m).

❾ THORNTHWAITE GALLERY

A 300-year-old building displaying works for sale by local artists. In summer there are craft demonstrations. Tearoom. (Open mid Mar–Nov, Wed–Mon; Dec–Feb Fri, Sat and Sun. ☕ ♿. Phone 017687 78248) Northwest of the Swan Hotel is the Bishop of Barf, a 7 foot (2 m) high whitewashed rock.

❿ WHINLATTER VISITOR CENTRE

The main feature is an exhibition which tells the story of the forest. There are also displays, picnic facilities, refreshments and a forest trail. The top of Whinlatter Pass offers superb views. (Open daily ☕. Phone 017687 78469)

⓫ WHITEHAVEN

This was one of England's busiest ports in the 18th century and a target of pirates. There are some superb Georgian buildings; look at the houses at the point where Roper Street meets Scotch Street, or at the church. The Museum and Art Gallery in the Civic Hall has model ships, mining displays and lots of gruesome detail about a very well preserved 14th-century battle casualty who was dug up at St Bees. (Open Mon–Sat) Michael Moon's bookshop (Roper Street) is a mecca for many, with room for 100 browsers and one mile of shelving. (Open Mon–Sat ♿. Phone 01946 62936) ☎ 01946 695678

⓬ WORKINGTON

This maritime and coal town's most famous visitor was Mary Queen of Scots, who stopped over at Workington Hall after fleeing Scotland in 1568. A series of storyboards helps you explore what remains of this once great country house. (Open Easter–Oct, Tues–Fri; Sat–Sun, afternoons only) For local history, go to the small Helena Thompson Museum in Park End Road. (Open Mon–Sat. Phone 01900 62598)

The Northern Lakes

Preceding page: Early morning, Derwentwater

Moot Hall, Keswick

Watendlath

St John's Vale, Keswick

Thirlmere

Judith Parr's House, Watendlath

Many visitors choose to use this area as their base for exploring the whole of the Lake District. Quite simply, for most Lakeland enthusiasts Derwentwater is *the* lake, Langdale *the* valley and Watendlath *the* hamlet. The scenery is classic too – the north dominated by the rounded slopes of the Skiddaw range, and the south by the craggy, wild central Lakeland mountains.

The town of Keswick separates the two distinctive areas of Skiddaw and Borrowdale. Skiddaw, the region's third highest peak (3053 ft/931 m) lies just a few miles north of Keswick. The 'grandpa' mountain of the Skiddaw slate group, it is composed of softer, crumblier rock than that found to the south at Borrowdale, where the brasher, newer, tougher volcanic rocks dominate the heart of Lakeland.

These newer rocks, forced up by heat, are rich in minerals. The discovery of one of the strangest of them, graphite, led to the development of the pencil industry in the area. The graphite was made by a process involving trees being caught in lava and then crushed for many millions of years. Some people say it's a pity the process didn't continue a bit longer and produce diamonds instead! All the same, graphite has turned out to be of tremendous importance to the area. At first no one could work out how it might be used. The locals tried burning it, with little success, then they marked sheep with it instead. Later it was found to be just the thing for dusting your cannonball moulds if you wanted the casting to come out perfectly. Others swore by it as a sure cure for all sorts of digestive problems. The demand for graphite eventually became so great that, by 1788, it was fetching over £3,300 a ton. It was said that a mouthful of 'wad' (the local name for the mineral) smuggled out of the mine would buy you drinks for a week at the Queen's Hotel in Keswick. When graphite was sent to London, it was by armed stagecoach. Someone eventually discovered that graphite is ideal as a writing and drawing material and, as a result, a thriving cottage industry in artists' pencils sprang up in Keswick. The pencil industry still goes on in the town. The mining of graphite, though, sharply declined after 1795 when a way was found of manufacturing the mineral artificially.

Ironically, Keswick also has a close association with an organization that's about as far removed from mining as you can get – the National Trust. Canon Rawnsley, the local vicar, was one of the

Castlerigg Stone Circle, Keswick

Crossthwaite church, Keswick

Derwentwater from Cat Bells

founder-members of the Trust, which he helped to set up in 1895. He was the Trust's honorary secretary until his death in 1920. Rawnsley fought tirelessly to get the 195 acres of Brandelhow Woods and Fell for the Trust in 1901, raising £7,000 in five months. This was the first National Trust property in the Lakes. In 1922 Friar's Crag and the surrounding area were bought as a memorial to the canon. Since this time the Trust's landholdings in the area have grown to include most of the central fell area, almost all the major valley heads, six of the main lakes, 86 farms, several campsites, numerous car parks and, last

Barrow Bay, Derwentwater

Nichol End, Derwentwater

Jaws of Borrowdale, Derwentwater

but by no means least, a cottage with an earth privy. (The cottage is being preserved and is let to visiting tourists.)

Unfortunately, Canon Rawnsley didn't win all his battles. Despite the help of such heavyweight contemporaries as William Morris, John Ruskin and Thomas Carlyle, Rawnsley couldn't prevent Manchester Corporation passing a law (1879) which allowed the water level of the two natural lakes of Thirlmere to be raised by 54 feet (16 m) and turned the area into one vast reservoir. The project flooded the old road and the hamlets of Armboth and Wythburn. Also lost was the bridge

which joined the two lakes and which the poets Coleridge and Wordsworth had often used as a meeting point. Wythburn church – a favourite spot from which to start the climb up Helvellyn – survives. You can see pictures of the area as it looked before the flooding at the King's Arms pub at Thirlspot.

The locals were even less happy in 1908 when the hillsides were densely planted with conifers to control soil erosion and the speed that rainfall ran off into the lake. More recently the North-West Water Authority (the new owners) have been planting native trees again and allowing people

John Peel's grave, Caldbeck

Snow-capped Skiddaw

Little Langdale Tarn

Ashness Bridge

both around and on the reservoir, so Thirlmere is coming to life again.

Hunting is a favourite pastime in the region. Britain's most famous huntsman, John Peel, lived and died in Caldbeck, a village the other side of the Skiddaw range from Keswick. He's best remembered as the hero of the song, 'D'ye ken John Peel' (1828/9), which was written one snowy afternoon by Peel's friend John Graves, whose daughter wanted to know the words to a song her grandmother was singing. Graves did no more than pen a new set of words in honour of his friend, who was with him at the time. Graves's old house is marked with a plaque to commemorate the event. The song was given its first public airing in the Rising Sun Inn, Caldbeck, now called the Oddfellows' Arms.

Caldbeck

Whatever your views on foxhunting, Peel was a bit of a character. A big man (over 6 ft/1.8 m tall and weighing about 13 stones/86.5 kg), he had a large nose, tremendously long legs and very sharp grey eyes. 'His coat so grey' was, of course, made of local undyed Herdwick wool. After eloping to Gretna Green, he spent the rest of his life neglecting his family and farm for the greater pleasures of the hunt and hostelry. One less than complimentary local described him as, 'Nobbut a drunken old tagglet'. Maybe he had some excuse, though. After all, Caldbeck did have 13 pubs in those days.

Peel hunted foxes obsessively. On one occasion, he's reputed to have gone on for 10 hours 40 minutes without a break – all in vain, though, because his quarry escaped. Peel died as he had lived – hunting.

21

❶ BLEA TARN

There are several small, picturesque lakes called Blea Tarn in the Lake District. Wordsworth loved this particular Blea Tarn, and you can walk right round it. In *The Excursion* he wrote:

'Full many a spot
Of hidden beauty have I chanced to espy
Among the mountains; never one like this;
So lonesome, and so perfectly secure.'

❷ BORROWDALE

This valley lies just to the south of Derwentwater. Don't miss the exceptionally pretty village of Grange. Near here the valley narrows into the 'Jaws of Borrowdale' and to the west is the easily accessible Castle Crag viewpoint. To the east you'll find the massive Bowder Stone. It looks as though it's about to topple over any minute, but don't worry – it's been keeping its balance since the Ice Age! The stone is 36 feet (11 m) high, 62 feet (19 m) long, weighs about 2000 tons (2032 tonnes), and you can climb to the top of it.

❸ CALDBECK

This was the stamping ground of the huntsman John Peel. Born at Park End, Caldbeck, in 1776, he was finally laid to rest in Caldbeck churchyard in 1854. His gravestone, decorated with hunting motifs, is still there. Also in Caldbeck you'll find Priest's Mill, an 18th-century watermill with its machinery fully restored and in working order. There's a small mining museum and a coffee shop here too. (Open mid Mar–Oct, Tues–Sun; Nov–Dec, Sat and Sun only ♿. Phone 016974 78369)

❹ CASTLERIGG STONE CIRCLE

It is not known why the present 38 boulders were erected some 3500 years ago in this superb setting. The 'circle' is actually an oval, 107 feet (33 m) across at its broadest point. ♿

❺ DERWENTWATER

A favourite with many people, this lake can be explored by launch from Lakeside. Alternatively, you can walk on just a bit farther south to Friar's Crag, where you'll find what John Ruskin considered to be one of the finest views in Europe. Castle Head, just north-east of here (across the B5289), also offers a rewarding view.

❻ KESWICK

The town's four museums provide plenty of variety. Cars for the Stars features the motors of Del Boy, Bergerac, James Bond and the Saint. (Open Mar–Dec daily. Phone 01768 75757 ♿ ☎) Beatrix Potter's Lake District (off Market Place) is an audiovisual display about the children's writer's life as a farmer and conservationist. (Open Apr–Oct daily, Nov–Mar, Sat and Sun. Phone 017687 75173) The Cumberland Pencil Museum (Greta Bridge) tells the story of pencils through the ages. Exhibits include the world's longest pencil, at 7 feet (2 m). (Open daily ♿ ☎) The Keswick Museum and Art Gallery (Fitz Park) houses the original manuscript of *Goldilocks and the Three Bears*, as well as weird curiosities such as a 500-year-old mummified cat and the so-called musical stones, a 12 foot (3.5 m) long musical instrument you can have a bash at playing. (Open Apr–Oct, Mon–Sat ♿) ☎ 017687 72645

❼ LANGDALE

This popular area has lovely scenery and many enjoyable walks. Most visitors head west from Great Langdale and stop at either the National Trust car park for Stickle Ghyll or the car park by the New Dungeon Ghyll Hotel to explore both waterfalls. Stickle Ghyll Force drops 128 feet (38 m) onto boulders. Dungeon Ghyll Force is named after the black chasm that the waterfall (52 ft/16 m) plunges into. Farther up the valley is Old Dungeon Ghyll Hotel, which was given to the National Trust by the famous historian G. M. Trevelyan. If you're not feeling very energetic but want a bit of peace and quiet, try walking up the valleys of Mickleden Beck or Oxendale Beck. Behind Fell Foot Farm, in Little Langdale (on the way to Wrynose Pass), there's a flat-topped mound with steps leading up to it. This is thought to be a Thing Mount or Assembly Mound for the Vikings who once ruled this area.

❽ LINGHOLM

Lingholm has impressive formal gardens, woodland and great views. Beatrix Potter's family used the house as a holiday home for a few years and Lingholm itself crops up in many of the writer's tales. Tearooms and plant centre. (Open Apr–Oct daily ♿. Phone 017687 72003) Lingholm Woods were Squirrel Nutkin's home. Just north, at Fawe Park, is Benjamin Bunny country. To the south is Newlands Valley and the setting for Mrs Tiggy-Winkle. She lived up the side of Cat Bells, a popular fell walk. This is best reached from Gutherscale car park (just north-east of Skelgill), or from Hawse End Pier, which connects with the Derwentwater launch.

❾ LODORE FALLS

You'll find these next to the Swiss Lodore Hotel. Small cascades splash through rocks in the woods and then drop 40 feet (12 m). If you want to see the falls 'smiting and fighting', in Robert Southey's memorable words, make sure you visit them after heavy rainfall. Barely a mile north of here is a side road leading to Ashness Bridge, Surprise View and Watendlath (the tiny, isolated village that was the home of Hugh Walpole's Judith Paris). All three are beauty spots and consequently are crowded in summer. Leave your car behind and use the Derwentwater launch instead; this will set you down at Ashness Bridge Pier.

❿ THIRLMERE

This reservoir serves Manchester, some 96 miles (150 km) away, and stretches along the main Keswick to Grasmere road. The road along the west side is the more peaceful route. There are good viewpoints at Raven Crag (north-west end of the lake) and Hause Point (a promontory two-thirds of the way along the lake). Between them lies Launchy Ghyll Forest Trail and its 100 foot (30 m) high waterfall.

Wordsworth Country

Stone bear, Dacre churchyard

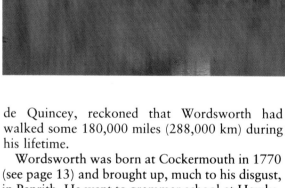

Preceding page: Gowbarrow Bay, Ullswater   Dacre Castle

The name of the poet William Wordsworth is inextricably linked to the heart of Lakeland. He spent his whole life here and drew inspiration for his greatest works from it. The Lakes have a literary tradition that begins with Wordsworth and continues to this day.

The classic portrait of Wordsworth has him walking for miles through the Lakeland countryside – with his favourite mountain, Helvellyn, in the background – composing at the top of his voice. One of the poet's friends, the writer Thomas de Quincey, reckoned that Wordsworth had walked some 180,000 miles (288,000 km) during his lifetime.

Wordsworth was born at Cockermouth in 1770 (see page 13) and brought up, much to his disgust, in Penrith. He went to grammar school at Hawkshead (see page 77) and then on to be a lazy undergraduate at St John's College, Cambridge. By 1791 he'd become a radical as a result of his visits to revolutionary France.

Wordsworth and his sister Dorothy went to live

Rydal Water

Brotherswater Inn

Loughrigg Tarn, near Ambleside

at Dove Cottage, Grasmere, in 1799. Life was quite hard at this time – porridge was often on the menu and newspaper served as wallpaper. When their financial situation eventually eased, William married his sweetheart, Mary (1802). The wedding left his sister in a state of collapse. 'Poor Miss Wordsworth', as she was called locally, later went mad. William, in contrast, faired considerably better. It was at this time that he started producing some of his best work, including *Daffodils*; in fact, for this poem William drew on raw material supplied by Dorothy, who had kept detailed descriptions of the flowers they had seen during a walk two years earlier.

The Dove Cottage era ended in 1808 when William and his growing family moved to Allan Bank, also in Grasmere. They all hated it. The house was cold and the chimneys smoked; William called it 'a temple of abomination'. (Allan Bank was given to the National Trust by Canon Rawnsley but is not open to the public.) Understandably, the family soon moved again, in 1811, 27

View across Ullswater to Gowbarrow Fell

Ullswater

Grasmere

Outward Bound School sailing boat, Ullswater

Clappersgate Bridge, near Ambleside

28

Dove Cottage

but their choice was not a fortunate one. The damp Grasmere parsonage was the scene of the deaths of Catherine and Thomas, two of the Wordsworths' five children. Two years later, in 1813, the family settled in Rydal Mount, a short distance from the parsonage. William, now financially secure in a government job as distributor of stamps, parted company with his radical past. He returned to the fold of the Anglican church and the establishment, becoming a Tory, opposing the 1832 Reform Bill and eventually, in 1843, becoming Poet Laureate. He died on 23 April 1850 – Shakespeare's birthday and also St George's day.

The tradition of rushbearing dates back to the days when churches had earth floors covered with rushes. Once a year the rushes were changed – no doubt greatly improving the odour of sanctity. The churches in the area now have tiled or flagged floors, but several communities continue to mark the occasion. The modern version of this ancient

Ullswater from near Howtown

ceremony is a much grander affair than the original. In Grasmere and Ambleside, for example, it's a great family occasion complete with processions and bands.

Grasmere Rushbearing is on the Saturday nearest 5 August (St Oswald's Day). Ambleside Rushbearing is a movable feast but is usually held on the first or second Saturday in July. Warcop, Musgrave and Urswick also hold rushbearings. If you can't arrange to see one, have a look at the mural in Ambleside Church for a glimpse of the proceedings.

Children who attend Rushbearing at Grasmere and Ambleside are given pieces of the region's

Martindale

Ambleside by Stock Ghyll

Aira Force, Ullswater

Water wheel at Stock Ghyll

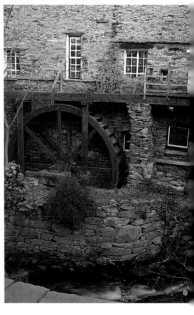

Glenridding Pier, Ullswater

Pooley Bridge, Ullswater

spicy gingerbread, which is a bread- or cake-like sweet rather than a biscuit.

Such a diet would undoubtedly help you to become as large as a certain George Steadman, though whether you would be as fit is another matter. Steadman was fourteen times heavyweight champion in Cumberland and Westmorland wrestling at the Grasmere Games in the 19th century. His chest measured 51 inches (128 cm) across and his calves were almost 18 inches (47 cm) round. This type of wrestling is similar to sumo. The two opponents clasp hands behind each other's back and necks and try to force each other to touch the ground or release the hand-hold. Bouts are generally won with a crafty flick, so agility and intelligence are needed more than brute force and weight. The various flicks have wonderful names such as the hank, the swing hype or the cross-buttock. The last of these terms was invented by the rector of Egremont! To add to the spectacle the wrestlers wear what looks like thermal underwear topped with velvet knickers. Hot stuff on a summer's day.

An equally strenuous Lakeland summer sport is fell running, which involves running up and down a mini mountain. The fell-running competition held at Grasmere is called the 'guides race'. Contestants have to leap down scree, scramble over walls and scratch themselves skinless on the heather. Great fun!

If that doesn't appeal, why not try hound trailing instead? This is designed to let man's best friend do the hard part and leave you to pick up the prize and the praise at the end. The hounds are specially bred and fed for the event; the diet being a closely guarded secret. To make them eager, they are starved for the 24 hours immediately prior to the race. The race begins when the hounds are let loose (or given 'the slip') to follow a specially laid paraffin and aniseed trail. This may wend and wind for up to 8 miles (12 km) before leading them back to the start. The owners are in a frenzy of excitement during the closing stages of the race, their enthusiasm no doubt fuelled by the bets that hang on the result.

This and similar traditional sports are held at Ambleside on the Thursday before the first Monday in August. At Grasmere on the third Thursday after the first Monday in August, you can enjoy high leaping, long leaping and flat racing. If you find it too complicated working out the date, phone the Tourist Information Centre!

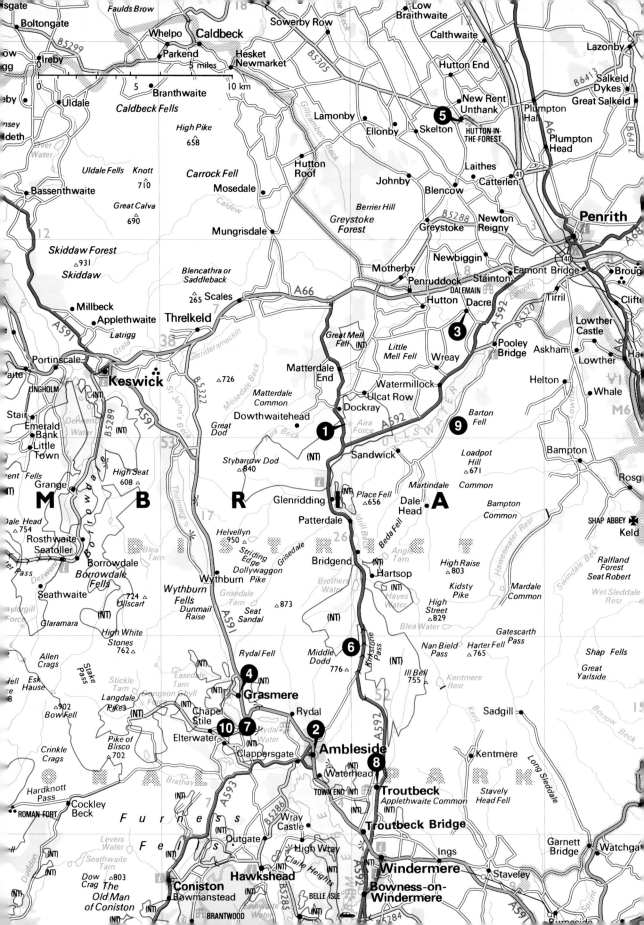

❶ | AIRA FORCE

This famous 70 foot (21 m) high waterfall belonging to the National Trust stands in the grounds of the Victorian-landscaped Gowbarrow Park.

❷ | AMBLESIDE

Recent traffic-calming measures in Ambleside mean that the village's many delights can now be enjoyed in some degree of comfort. A unique and valuable collection of literature, the Armitt Collection, can be seen in a special section of the public library. (Open Mon– Wed and Fri) The art of glass-blowing is demonstrated at Adrian Sankey's Glass. (Open daily &) Nearby and perched precariously over the rushing waters of Stock Ghyll is Bridge House (c. 1650). In the 1850s Mr and Mrs Rigg and their six children lived here – some feat considering that the main room of the tiny one-up, one-down summer-house measures only 13 ft by 6 ft (4 m by 1.9 m)! Now the building is home to a National Trust shop and information centre. A walk to north-east Ambleside will take you to the 90 foot (27 m) Stock Ghyll Force waterfall. South-west of Ambleside are the foundations of a Roman fort, Galava. South-east of the town is Stagshaw Gardens, a National Trust property over-looking Windermere. (Open Apr– Jun daily; Jul–end Oct by appoint-ment only. Phone 015394 35599) Behind the gardens stands the Jenkin Crag viewpoint (750 ft/ 230 m), which can be reached from Ambleside. ☎ 015394 32582

❸ | DACRE

This village is steeped in church history; in AD 731 Bede wrote of a monastery in the village. The pre-sent church is Norman. In the churchyard are four weird carvings of bears. From the churchyard you can also see the 14th-century Dacre Castle, which is said to be haunted but, unfortunately, is not open to the public.

❹ | GRASMERE

You'll find plenty to do here. To the south-east of the village you'll find Dove Cottage and the Words-worth Museum. William's years spent here (1799–1808) were the happiest and most productive of his life. Manuscripts, paintings, displays on local life and a mock-up of an old farmhouse interior are just some of the features. (Open daily; closed Jan. &) In the village centre is St Oswald's Church, where you will find the graves of William, his wife Mary and his sister Dorothy. Nearby is Sarah Nelson's gingerbread shop – sweet-toothed visitors won't be able to pass by without sampling Sarah's famous recipe. Heaton Cooper Studio has an exhibition of paint-ings, including many watercolours of the lakes and mountains. (Open daily. Phone 015394 35280 &) Demonstrations of handloom weaving can be seen at Reekie's Limited. (Open daily &) If you want a breath of fresh air, head north-west out of the town towards Easedale. This will bring you up past the waterfall of Sour Milk Ghyll to Easedale Tarn. From here you can make an ascent up Helm Crag (1299 ft/396 m). ☎ 015394 35245

❺ | HUTTON-IN-THE-FOREST

This was reputedly the home of Sir Gawain's Green Knight, one of the characters in the tales of King Arthur and the Knights of the Round Table. More recently, since 1600, it has been the home of the Inglewood family. Although part of the house dates from the 1300s, the interior is Victorian. Outside there is a terrace of topiary, a walled garden, a forest walk and landscaped parkland. (House and tearoom open May–Oct, Thurs, Fri, Sun and Bank Hols and Weds in Aug. Grounds open all year, Sun–Fri. Phone 017684 84449)

❻ | KIRKSTONE PASS

There are two routes leading up to the pass (1489 ft/454 m): one via an A road from Troutbeck and one via a steeper, unclassified road (called the Struggle) from Amble-side. Both routes provide good views. Just before you reach the top of the pass, you'll come to the Kirkstone Pass Inn, which has the distinction of holding third place in the altitude ratings for English pubs. The pass owes its name to a rock at the top which looks like a church steeple. The road to Ulls-water takes you past the lake of Brotherswater, allegedly named after two brothers who drowned here in a skating accident. Patter-dale, a village famous for its late-summer sheepdog trials, stands almost at the edge of the lake.

❼ | RYDAL WATER

This small lake has a Wordsworth haven to the north-east of it, Rydal Mount. The only colour portrait of the poet's sister, Dorothy, hangs in the house. The garden was planned by Wordsworth himself. (Open daily. Phone 015394 33002)

❽ | TROUTBECK

The main attraction of this village, apart from its setting, is Town End. Built about 1626 by a yeoman farmer called George Browne, this house was lived in by successive generations of the Browne family until 1944. It is full of the family's furniture, tools and artefacts. (Open Apr–Nov, Tues–Fri, Sun and Bank Hols. Phone 015394 32628) If you head south along the main valley road you'll come to Holehird Gardens, which has fine displays of azaleas, rhododendrons, alpine plants and heathers. (Open daily &.)

❾ | ULLSWATER

You can take a cruise on the second-largest lake (7 miles/11 km long) in the area aboard either *Lady of the Lake* (1877) or *Raven* (1889), both operated by the Ullswater Naviga-tion and Transit Company Ltd (of Kendal). Services run daily (early Apr–Oct &) from Glenridding to Howtown and then on to Pooley Bridge. Phone 017684 82229. ☎ 017684 82414

❿ | WHITE MOSS COMMON

This area lies between Grasmere and Rydal. A path leads from the car park to the River Rothay. Across the river you'll find a nature trail and paths leading to Lough-rigg Terrace viewpoint and, for the energetic, on to Loughrigg Fell (1101 ft/336 m).

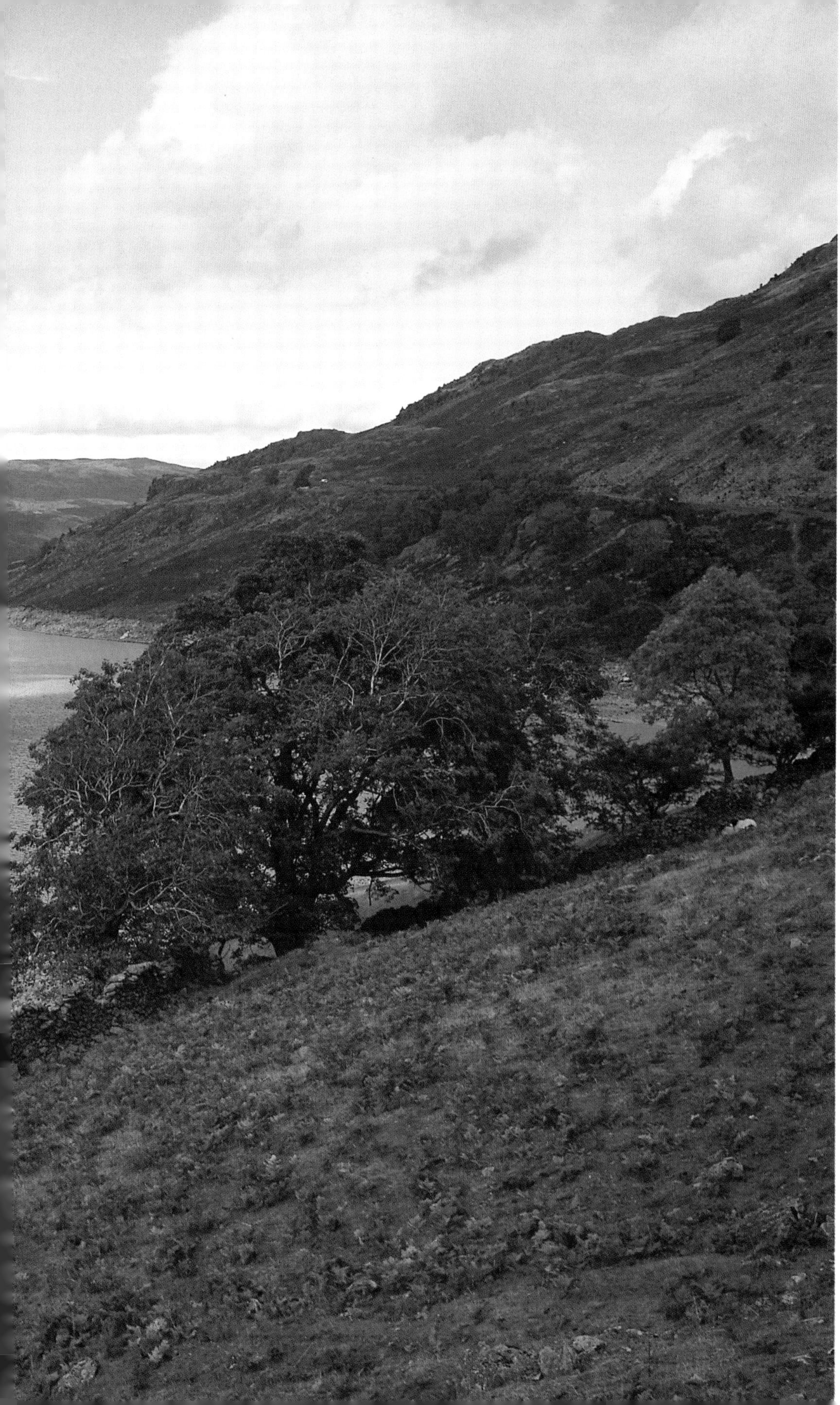

The North-East Lakes

Bridge at Lazonby

Pele church tower, Great Salkeld

Preceding page: **Haweswater from Mardale Common**

The old red sandstone town of Penrith is a wonderful centre for the visitor to this part of Lakeland. To the east and north there's the lush Eden valley; to the south there are many pretty limestone villages which gradually give way before the wilds near the summit of Shap's granite; and to the west scenery dominated by craggy volcanic rock.

Peace and quiet are, of course, just the thing for wildlife and especially birdlife. In the woods around Haweswater you'll find woodpeckers, pied flycatchers, redstarts, tree pipits and wood warblers, while by the lakeside itself there are dippers, grey wagtails and common sandpipers.

Up on the fells, wheatears and ring ouzels nest. Of the predators, there are sparrowhawks, buzzards, peregrine falcons and ravens, and the occasional golden eagle. In Haweswater itself there is an unusual silver fish called the schelly which grows to about 12 inches (31 cm) and is sometimes called the freshwater herring; other than here the schelly is only found in Ullswater and Red Tarn on Helvellyn. The char, a relation of the trout, is another regional rarity. On land, keep your eyes open for red squirrels, the shy roe deer, red deer and otters, which are making a comeback after a prolonged period of low numbers.

The region has a wide variety of plantlife.

Blacksmith's forge, Penrith Steam Museum

Dalemain House

Long Meg and Her Daughters, Little Salkeld

Alpines can be found high up on the mountains. It may seem curious that flowers are more scarce on the milder lower fells, but the competition from sheep and bracken can be too much, especially as the soil is often poor. In damp spots you may find plants that overcome this problem, such as the white sundew or the violet butterwort; both feed by trapping insects. Lower down the hillsides is juniper and bilberry country.

Yellow was appropriately the favourite colour of one of the district's most flamboyant characters – 'Hughie', fifth Earl of Lonsdale between 1880 and 1944, and a member of the Lowther Clan. The Lowthers were granted lands in Lakeland by Edward I, in 1283, and went on to become tremendously wealthy; the development of Whitehaven was mainly due to their efforts. In the 1780s the family asked the Adam brothers to design Lowther village, intended to house their estate workers, but the project was only partially completed. Lowther Castle, near Penrith, was another matter. This enterprise cost £60,000 and the remains of Shap Abbey, which was plundered for building stone. The house had an imposing 420-foot (128 m) frontage and was in the Gothic style. Such a grand setting called for grand entertaining and grand spending. Hughie was certainly equal to the task. His guest list included Edward VII and

Askham church

Howtown

Lowther Park

the Kaiser. Sixty servants would be on hand to wait on these and other illustrious visitors. It's hardly surprising that Hughie's annual expenditure in 1910 was £180,000.

The sport-mad Hughie became internationally famous when he challenged and subsequently beat the then world heavyweight boxing champion, John L. Sullivan. He was famous at home, too – for instituting the yellow Lonsdale Belt awarded in boxing, and for travelling in style in a yellow

Wet Sleddale Reservoir, Shap

Shap Abbey

Rolls-Royce and attended by yellow-liveried servants. Hughie was the Automobile Association's first president, hence the yellow uniform which was chosen in deference to him.

The 1930s saw a dramatic slump in the family's traditional source of income, coal mining, but no corresponding decrease in Hughie's spending. By the time of his death, in 1944, the Lowthers' financial affairs were in a parlous state and it was not until James, the seventh Earl, succeeded to the title in 1953 that the family's fortunes began to pick up again. Indeed, James ended up one of the country's richest men.

Lowther Castle was damaged by fire in the 1950s and later demolished to leave what remains today, an empty shell. The present Lord Lonsdale lives down the road from the old house, in the Elizabethan Askham Hall.

Lady Anne Clifford is a similarly remarkable

Maulds Meaburn

Near St Andrew's churchyard, Penrith

Shop sign, Penrith

character who has left her mark on the region. Her one misfortune was in being born a woman in 17th-century England. Marriage to the spendthrift and philanderer Richard Sackville, Earl of Dorset, became one long battle of wits for what she regarded as her inheritance – large tracts of land in the region. Sackville was quite as eager as Anne's male relatives that she should renounce her claim, because he would then receive a much-needed injection of cash in compensation for the loss of the lands; in those days what was hers was, in fact, his! But Anne gamely stuck to her guns, despite emotional pressure by her husband, who denied her access to her only child, and hectoring by the Archbishop of Canterbury and King James I. Eventually, her claim was rejected and that seemed to be that. The unhappy Anne buried Richard and then married Philip Herbert (later Earl of Pembroke), who wasn't much of an improvement on her first husband. But, by 1650, Philip too was

Crosby Ravensworth

Lowther Castle

Brougham Castle

Countess's Pillar, near Brougham

dead and Anne's male relatives had died, leaving her free to head north and take possession of what she'd fought for in vain all those years ago. Her life from this point on was like that of a medieval prince and was spent rebuilding the Clifford castles. She did this with great style, travelling from castle to castle with a retinue of about 300 servants. Her great courage did not lessen with age either. She remained openly and defiantly Royalist when most people daren't even whisper criticism of the Roundheads. As you'd expect, her sense of honour was no less robust. It's said that a fellow called Murgatroyd once refused to hand over a hen in payment of rent that he owed to the Clifford estate. Anne spent £200 pursuing the stubborn Murgatroyd through the law courts. After winning the case, she promptly sweetened the pill for Murgatroyd by cooking the pricey hen and asking him to eat it with her. Anne Clifford died in Brougham Castle, near Penrith, in 1676, aged 86. 41

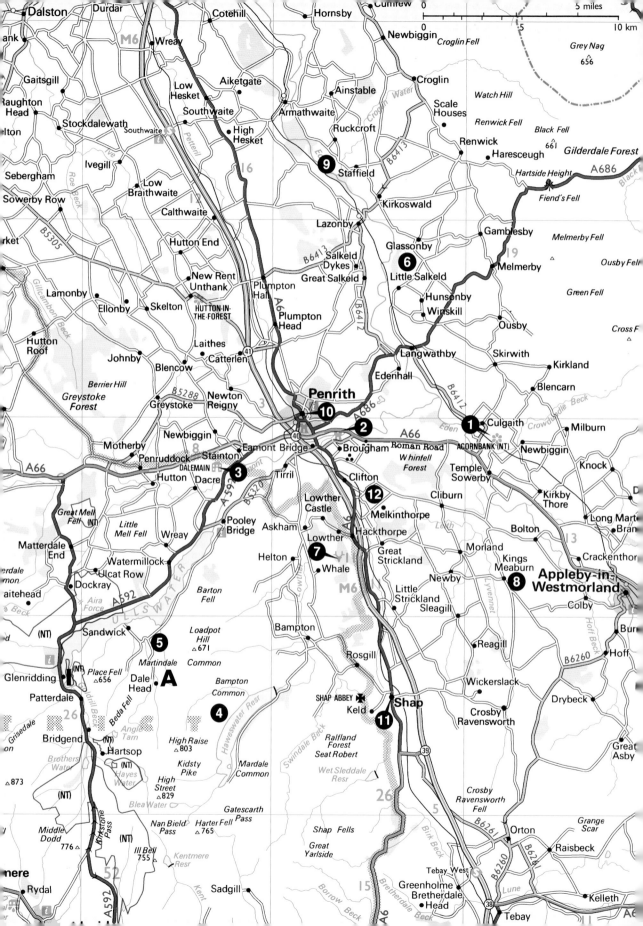

❶ ACORN BANK GARDEN

This 2¹/₂ acre (1 hectare) National Trust property lies about 6 miles (10 km) east of Penrith, at Temple Sowerby. Acorn Bank is noted for its herb garden; over 250 different varieties are grown here. (Open Apr–end Oct daily ♿. Phone 017683 61893)

❷ BROUGHAM CASTLE

The castle, pronounced 'Broom', stands 1¹/₂ miles (2.4 km) outside Penrith. Built in the early 1200s, it was one of the many castles restored in the 1600s by Lady Anne Clifford. It's in a super setting, on the River Eamont. You can climb the keep. There used to be a Roman fort nearby, hence the display of Roman tombstones. (Open Apr–Sept daily. Part ♿ ⚲. Phone 01768 862488) Close to the castle is the ruined Brougham Hall, now being restored and home to craft workshops. A mile east of the castle, on the A66, is the Countess's Pillar, which is decorated with brass sundials and commemorates the spot where Lady Anne Clifford last saw her mother alive.

❸ DALEMAIN

There's something for all the family at Dalemain House, which is part medieval, part Tudor and part Georgian. Inside the house you'll find fine paintings, furniture and an exotic Chinese Room, as well as displays on the local cavalry regiment, countryside and the local fell ponies. Outside there's a garden and adventure playground. (Open Easter–early Oct, Sun–Thurs ♿ ⚲. Phone 017684 86450)

❹ HAWESWATER

Another of the Lakeland reservoirs supplying Manchester, this one was begun in 1929 with the building of a 94 foot (29 m) high dam and the flooding of the village of Mardale; the latter makes the occasional unscheduled reappearance in very dry summers. This isolated part of Lakeland is ideal for wildlife. An RSPB observation post is open in summer, when golden eagles nest here. (Phone 01931 713337)

❺ HOWTOWN

Howtown is fabulous for walks. For an easy one-hour meander, take the footpath round Hallin Fell. If you don't mind a short sharp climb (about half an hour's worth) to a viewpoint, climb the 1271-foot (391 m) fell itself. This is reached from the south side via a footpath which starts near the car parks by Martindale new church (between Howtown and Martindale). For a more energetic walk taking about four hours, leave your car at Glenridding, cross to Howtown by steamer and then return via the footpath that skirts the shores of Ullswater. An alternative circular walk involves parking the car at Martindale, walking up Boardale and over the pass at the top. You return north-west along the Ullswater shore path.

❻ LONG MEG AND HER DAUGHTERS

These form a massive (c. 300 ft/92 m) stone circle. Long Meg is a 15 foot (4.5 m) tall standing stone. Twenty-seven of her original 66 'daughters' surround her. Legend has it that they were all turned to stone for dancing on Sundays!

❼ LOWTHER LEISURE PARK

All the fun of the fair in a 150 acre (61 hectare) parkland setting. The many attractions include a circus, a BMX bike track, a deer park, an assault course, a boating lake, a miniature railway and an archery area. Many of the sights are under cover. The Lowther Horse Driving Trials and Country Fair are also held in Lowther in early August. (Open Easter hols daily; mid Apr–Spring Bank Hol, weekends only; Spring Bank Hol–early Sept daily ♿ ⚲. Phone 01931 712523)

❽ MAULDS MEABURN

This is a particularly beautiful village about 4 miles (6 km) east of Shap and well worth a visit.

❾ NUNNERY WALKS

The Walks are delightful if you are in the mood for a peaceful amble. They consist of 2 miles (3 km) of paths which take you through unspoilt woodland by the River Eden and then on to the waterfalls at the sandstone gorge of the River Croglin. Tearoom. (Open daily ♿). The nearest village to the Walks is Kirkoswald, about 2 miles (3 km) away. St Oswald's Church stands in a hollow and over a well worshipped by pre-Christians. The bell tower was built on a hill nearby in an attempt to solve the problem of the sound of the bells not carrying.

❿ PENRITH

One of the features of this border town is the ruined castle which stands in the public park. The small Penrith Museum (Middlegate), formerly a school (c. 1670), provides a history of the area for visitors. (Open Easter–Oct daily; Nov–Mar, Mon–Sat). The Steam Museum (Castlegate) has displays of working engines and traction engines, a blacksmith's forge and a restored Victorian cottage. (Open Easter then Spring Bank Hol–Sept, Mon–Fri. Closed Sat and Sun ♿ ⚲) Penrith Beacon (937 ft/288 m) is a great viewpoint.

One mile south of Penrith are two prehistoric monuments which provide evidence of the area's importance as a religious centre in years past. Arthur's Round Table is a henge (a bank with a ditch on the *inside*). Mayburgh Earthwork is a bank of cobbles rising to 15 feet (4.6 m) and surrounding a 1¹/₂ acre (0.6 hectare) area. Within this ring there is one 9 foot (2.75 m) standing stone (the last stone in a circle of stones). (♿ to Arthur's Round Table) ☎ 01768 867466

⓫ SHAP

The ruined abbey hidden in the Lowther Valley to the west of Shap was originally founded in 1199. The ground plan is quite obvious from what remains, and the tower (c. 1500) survives well. (♿) Just south-east is the hamlet of Keld, where a small and very plain chapel of the 1400s (now belonging to the National Trust) speaks volumes about how poor and basic life was in the area.

⓬ WEATHERIGGS POTTERY

The pottery has been working since 1855 and has a museum, old machinery and demonstrations in pottery-making and weaving. (Open daily ♿. Phone 01768 892733)

South-West Lakeland

Preceding page: Wastwater

Wasdale Head

Muncaster Castle

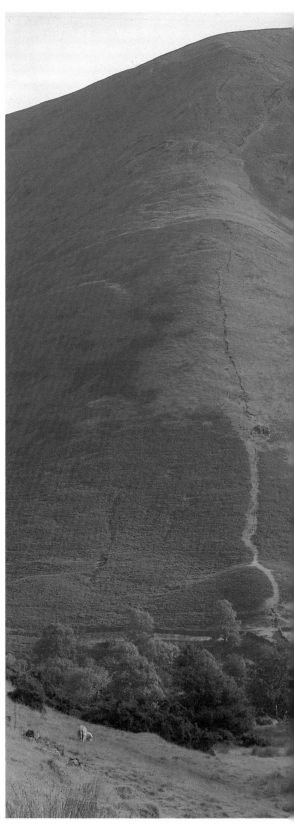

Wasdale Head Inn

This region is a mixture of natural scenic beauty and manmade landmarks. At one extreme there's Wastwater, one of the deepest and wildest lakes in England, and at the other, Sellafield – probably the most controversial industrial plant in the country. The varied scenery ranges from high volcanic crags, through granite dales to seaside sand-dunes. Settlements range from tiny, isolated sheep-farming hamlets to sleepy coastal villages. It's a surprising and largely unspoilt area.

Evidence of the area's industrial past is everywhere. The earliest miners in the region were the Romans, who produced smelted iron in Eskdale. Later, in the 1300s, the monks turned their hands to it, very successfully too. Hodbarrow used to be the world's largest iron-ore mine. The blood-red ore haematite was discovered here in 1843 and by the 1860s 265 men were at work underground.

Woodland by Wastwater

Twenty years later, production was running at over 340,000 tons (345,474 tonnes) per annum. Millom was built around 1865 to house the miners and their families. Great barriers were also put up to keep the sea out of the workings and to help the men mine under the sea itself. One of these barriers is over a mile long.

Farther up the coast the Ravenglass and Eskdale railway was built to serve the Nab Gill mines at Boot. This mine was much less successful than Hodbarrow and in 1912 it was flooded out. The 3-foot (90 cm) industrial gauge was then changed to the present 15-inch (37.5 cm) gauge to fit Mr Bassett-Lowke's model trains, which were tested here. The trains still worked, carrying granite from

47

Irton Cross, St Paul's churchyard

Murthwaite; some of this went into the concrete for London's Waterloo Bridge.

Watermills were built to provide the power for forging, fulling cloth, wood turning and, of course, grinding corn. It's not surprising that there are so many mills to visit in the district today.

Sellafield is one of the world's largest nuclear power plants. Originally called Windscale, the plant started up in 1951 to make plutonium for nuclear bombs. In 1956 the world's first industrial reactor was built here. Sellafield is now the world's largest nuclear reprocessing plant. In recent years it was the area's most visited tourist attraction, more popular even than Beatrix Potter's home.

Wastwater, whose lake bed is 58 ft/18 m below sea-level, is a product of the Ice Age when glaciers from the fells scooped out the valley and left in their place a cold, forbidding lake. This was originally filled with melted ice held in by a dam of debris that the glacier had deposited in the valley. The glacier couldn't escape and so pushed downwards, creating England's deepest lake.

Looking across Wastwater to Great Gable

Egremont Castle

Viking cross, Gosforth churchyard

Also in the valley of Wasdale are Scafell Pike, England's highest mountain; England's greatest liar, publican Will Ritson; and England's smallest church. The last claim is hotly disputed, but is valid if you work it out as cubic capacity for a used building.

Fell running is still a very popular sport among the locals and has produced some great Lakeland characters as well as remarkable achievements. One of the greatest of them all was the Lakeland guide Robert Graham. In 1932 Graham had set off from Keswick with the aim of running across the Lakeland peaks. He traversed nearly all of them in just under 23 hours 30 minutes. This was some performance and set a new record. The best known of recent fell runners is sheep farmer Joss Naylor, who is known locally as 'the flying shepherd'. Joss has traversed 72 Lakeland peaks (all above 2000 ft/610 m) in a time of 23 hours 11 minutes. This has involved running about 108 miles (173 km) and climbing c 40,000 feet (12,200 m). In other words he's climbed 10,972 feet

Shoreline, Wastwater

Evening, Wastwater

Sellafield nuclear plant

Ravenglass Station

Bridge Inn, Santon

(3352 m) higher than Everest. What's even more amazing is that Joss has had a bad back since the age of nine, and in recent years has had two discs removed. Surprising though it may seem, the fell running actually helps rather than aggravates this weakness. Joss was awarded the MBE in 1976.

Many of the district's place names owe their origins to the several different groups of invaders who settled here at various times over the centuries. After the Romans left Cumbria the Celts controlled the region, which they called 'Cymru' (meaning 'the people' or 'us'). Penrith is a Celtic name. The Celts were conquered by the Christian Anglians from across the Pennines. These people seem to have settled in the area's fertile lowlands and are thought to be responsible for the -ton ending in place names. South-west of Wastwater there's a village called Irton, complete with an Anglian cross in the churchyard.

The words 'beck' (stream), 'gill' (ravine) and 'pike' (pointed hilltop) are Norse (northern Viking). The Norsemen roamed far and wide through the region. Norse words and place names crop up all over and are more prevalent here than in any other area of Britain. The tangible evidence of the Viking presence, such as the Gosforth cross or the possible thing mound or parliament hill at Langdale, can seem so strange as to make it difficult for us to grasp the true extent of the Norsemen's influence. It's only when you start looking at the language and traditions of Cumbria that you realize how much of their culture the Norsemen left behind.

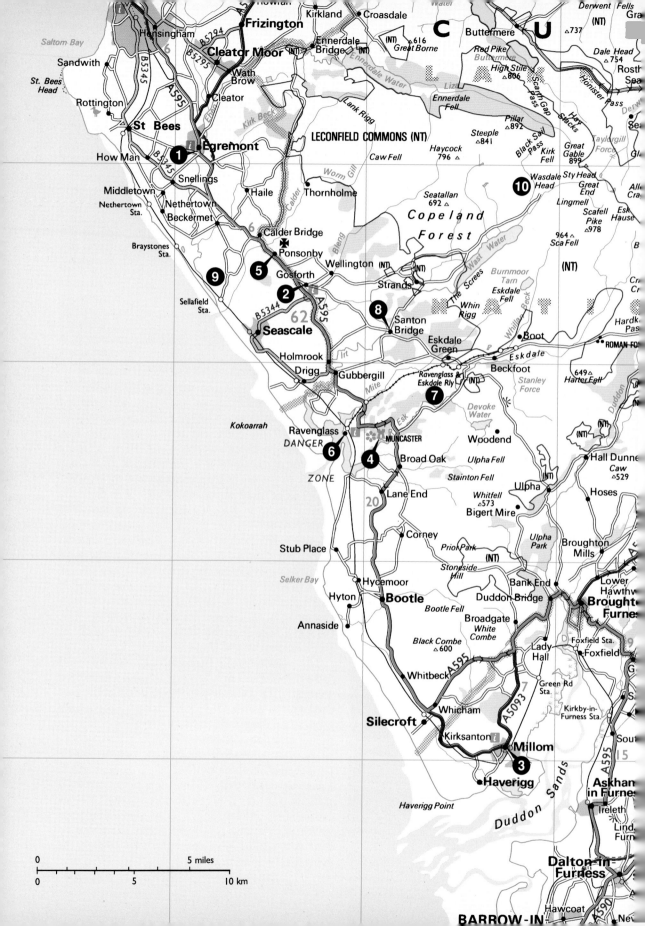

❶ EGREMONT

The main claim to fame of this small market town is the annual crab apple celebration, held in September since 1267. At noon a cartful of crab apples is thrown to the crowd, followed by track and field events and hound-trailing. In the evening there's a competition for making the ugliest face within the frame of a horse collar, called 'gurning through a braffin'. There's a pipe-smoking contest also, and a 30 foot (9 m) greasy pole to climb for the prize of a leg of lamb.

The more serious side of local life can be savoured in the 18th-century Lowes Court Gallery, which specializes in showing the works of local artists. (Open all year, Mon–Sat; closed Wed afternoon. Phone 01946 820693) In the town's public park you'll find a 12th-century pink sandstone castle. ☎ 01946 820693

❷ GOSFORTH

In the churchyard there is a beautifully preserved 14 foot (4 m) high Viking cross dating to c. AD 900. The slender column is carved with myths of the Norse gods and one image of the crucified Christ. A similar carved cross can be seen in the churchyard at Irton, south-east of Gosforth.

❸ MILLOM

The town of Millom overlooks the Duddon Estuary. The Folk Museum (St George's Road) has a display of the life and work of the Lakeland poet Norman Nicholson and reconstructions of a Victorian miner's kitchen and of the local iron ore mine. (Open Easter and Spring Bank Hol weeks then Whitsun–mid Sept, Mon–Sat ♿) The site of the mine is now part of the RSPB's Hodbarrow Nature Reserve. A 3 mile (5 km) public footpath runs round the lagoon, through the reserve and along the side of the sea wall.

❹ MUNCASTER CASTLE

This has been the home of the Pennington family since the 1200s. The oldest part of the castle, the pele tower, dates to 1345 but much of what you see today is Victorian. Inside, there are fine examples of 16th- and 17th-century furniture, tapestries and porcelain. Look out for the painting of Tom Skelton, the 16th-century fool of the Pennington family and the man after whom the word 'tomfoolery' was coined. Outside there are rhododendron and azalea gardens and wonderful views over the Esk Valley. You'll also find a commando course and World Owls – meet the birds daily at 2.30 pm. (Grounds open daily. Castle closed Mon and Nov–Mar. Phone 01229 717203)

❺ PONSONBY FARM PARK

This open farm has seven varieties of sheep, six of pig and four of cattle. There are three walking trails across the farm, as well as a farmyard to explore. The Farm Park also has a tearoom, picnic area, rabbit run, pets' corner and a children's play area. (Open Easter–Oct daily ♿. Phone 01946 841426)

Nearby is the ruined Calder Abbey (c. 1130); the site is on private land but is open to the public.

❻ RAVENGLASS

This town was a naval base in Roman times. The 12 foot (3.6 m) high walls of the old bath house, called Walls Castle, are all that remain from this period. Later Ravenglass became a centre for pearl-fishing and smuggling. These activities ended when the harbour silted up, creating dunes that now form part of the Eskmeals Nature Reserve. (Open all year; occasionally closes for gunnery practice. Always arrange in advance to visit Drigg Dunes Reserve. Phone 01298 23456)

❼ RAVENGLASS AND ESKDALE RAILWAY

Construction of England's oldest narrow-gauge system began in 1875. The present 15 inch (37.5 cm) gauge 'La'al Ratty' generally runs steam services on the 7 mile (11 km) long track up Eskdale. You can visit the railway's museum at Ravenglass station. There are tearooms at both Ravenglass and Eskdale termini. (Open Apr–Oct daily; Sat–Sun only in winter ♿ ♿ (Raven-glass) Phone 01229 717171)

Muncaster Mill, a 19th-century water-powered corn mill with working machinery, can be reached by taking the train from Ravenglass and getting off at a request stop one mile down the line. In addition to the mill itself, there's a pets' corner and picnic area. (Open Apr–Oct, Tues–Sun. Phone 01229 717614)

Eskdale Corn Mill, at Boot, is a water-powered mill with farming and milling exhibitions and a comfortable walk from the terminus at Eskdale. Refreshments are available and there's a car park. If you have time, visit St Catherine's Church at Boot for its attractive setting. (Open Apr–Oct, daily)

Stanley Ghyll, also called Dalegarth Falls, is a waterfall with three cascades, the largest of which is 37 feet (11 m). It's one mile south of Eskdale terminus, along a National Park nature trail.

❽ SANTON BRIDGE INN

This inn hosts the annual Greatest Liar Competition (third Thurs in Nov). The contest starts after a supper of tatie pot, which is a sort of lamb stew. Entrants must either be locals or foreigners and strictly amateur – politicians and lawyers aren't allowed to enter!

❾ SELLAFIELD

The exhibition centre shows videos, computer games and working models to explain the workings of the nuclear industry. There are also coach tours around the site. Refreshments are available. (Open daily ♿ ♿. Phone 019467 27027)

❿ WASDALE HEAD

This wild place is considered the cradle of British rock climbing, for it was here that Britain's first climbing association was set up. The rugged mountains above and behind Wastwater have claimed the lives of several mountaineers; their graves can be seen in the tiny church of St Olaf.

The Wasdale Head Inn is famous for having had Will Ritson (1808–90), Britain's greatest liar, as its landlord. Photographs of the old rogue still hang in the inn.

Coniston Water

Roa Island

Preceding page: **Furness Abbey, Barrow**

At one end of this diverse area you'll find rugged mountain passes and few inhabitants, and at the other the heavily industrial Barrow-in-Furness with a population of over 60,000. Between these two extremes are bustling market towns and a soft, sandy coastline. Among the many sites are monasteries and mineshafts, and fells, fortresses and nature reserves.

The Romans set up 20 forts in this area between AD 98 and 138 but left little evidence of their occupation and in some places stayed only a comparatively short time. The fort in Hardknott Pass, for example, was probably abandoned altogether after AD 197. It stands halfway between the Roman forts at Ambleside and Ravenglass, in a most inhospitable part of the region. The Roman soldiers posted here must have wondered which of their gods they had offended. The road built by the Romans to connect all three forts continued to Watercrook, near Kendal and, from there, joined the main road to Carlisle and Lowbarrow bridge, south of Tebay. An alternative route from

Ship Inn, Piel Island

Ulverston Sands

Cockley Beck Fell

Slate footpath sign

Ambleside leads to another fort at Brougham, near Penrith. This route was, and still is, quite spectacular. Called High Street, it runs along the ridge of mountains south of Ullswater. Brougham fort is fairly unusual among the Roman forts of central Lakeland in that there seems to have been a large civilian township (*vicus*) outside its walls.

If you're a good walker or climber the best place to start exploring the area is, quite literally, at the top, round Scafell Pike, England's highest mountain (3210 ft/978 m); this now belongs to the

57

Rail viaduct across Morecambe Bay

Brantwood

Drinking fountain, Dalton-in-Furness

Piel Castle, Piel Island

National Trust and was given in memory of the dead of World War I. An extraordinary character called Alfred Wainwright got to know Lakeland in precisely this way over forty years ago. Wainwright's lifelong love affair with the Lake District began when he holidayed there as a young man. Over ten years later he took a drop in salary and moved to Kendal in order to be nearer his beloved fells. In 1952 he decided to climb and record all the Lakeland fells and mountains. With the precision you'd expect of a man who was now Kendal's borough treasurer, Wainwright calculated that it would take him 13 years to complete his task – and it did. The results of his labours run into seven volumes, entitled *The Pictorial Guide to the Lakeland Fells*, and are invaluable to the serious walker or climber. The books are facsimiles of Wainwright's original manuscripts, handwritten and with his own pen and ink drawings as illustrations. All proceeds from the book are donated to Animal Rescue Cumbria, a charity which looks after stray dogs and cats. Wainwright's efforts were recognized with the award of an MBE. If you are interested in knowing more about his life, the museum at Brantwood has a small, permanent display devoted to him which includes his drawings, pipe and, predictably, boots and socks as exhibits.

If you want to experience the joys of fell walking, make sure that you go well prepared. Recommended items include light boots that support the ankles and have non-slip soles, a detailed map (preferably 1:25,000 scale) and a rucksack. The sack should contain vital items such as a torch, compass, whistle and emergency rations, in addition to extra clothing in case the weather worsens; take a sweater, socks and a hat as it can get very cold up there. Make sure you have windproof and waterproof clothing as well, including leggings. A successful expedition depends on good planning. Don't try to cover too many miles too quickly: two miles an hour is about right, and add an hour for every 1000 feet (305 m) you climb. Phone Lake District National Park Weatherline on **019687 75757** for a taped forecast. Plan, too, an alternative route, just in case mother nature springs a nasty and unexpected surprise. Lastly, let someone know where you are going and when you expect to return.

The great 19th-century art critic and art historian, John Ruskin was, like Alfred Wainwright, an 'outsider' who felt a strong

View from Broughton Fell

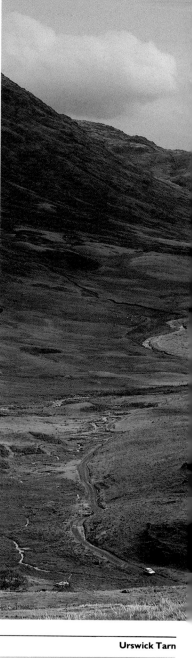

Urswick Tarn

affinity with Lakeland early in life. In Ruskin's case this was very early indeed; his first childhood memory was of walking with his nurse on Friar's Crag at Derwentwater, and at the age of five he had his first view of Coniston Water. Ruskin did not become a resident of Lakeland until 1871, some 47 years after his first visit, when he bought a house called Brantwood. The house stands at the edge of Coniston Water and is said to be the most beautifully situated in the whole of the Lake District. Ruskin must have been convinced of this claim because he happily paid £1500 without

Sir John Barrow memorial, Ulverston

Wrynose Bottom

Climbers at Hoad Hill, Ulverston

seeing the property. Visitors still marvel at the impressive setting and the wonderful lake and mountain views. Brantwood was Ruskin's base until he died, in 1900.

Although primarily remembered today for his influence in the field of art, Ruskin was also a tireless advocate of social justice and a vociferous critic of the adverse effects of industrialization; many of the 250 books written by him reflect these concerns. Ruskin wanted to help make the world a better place and art had a role in this. His defence of both Turner and the pre-Raphaelite Brother-

hood of artists in the face of widespread hostility to their work was based on an admiration of their purity of purpose as much as an appreciation of their respective techniques. Watercolours by Turner used to be a feature of Ruskin's bedroom at Brantwood and he owned several paintings by the pre-Raphaelites Burne-Jones and Holman-Hunt.

Ruskin himself was an accomplished water-colourist and a major expansion has taken place at Brantwood to cope with the 'bringing home' of his many paintings and drawings.

61

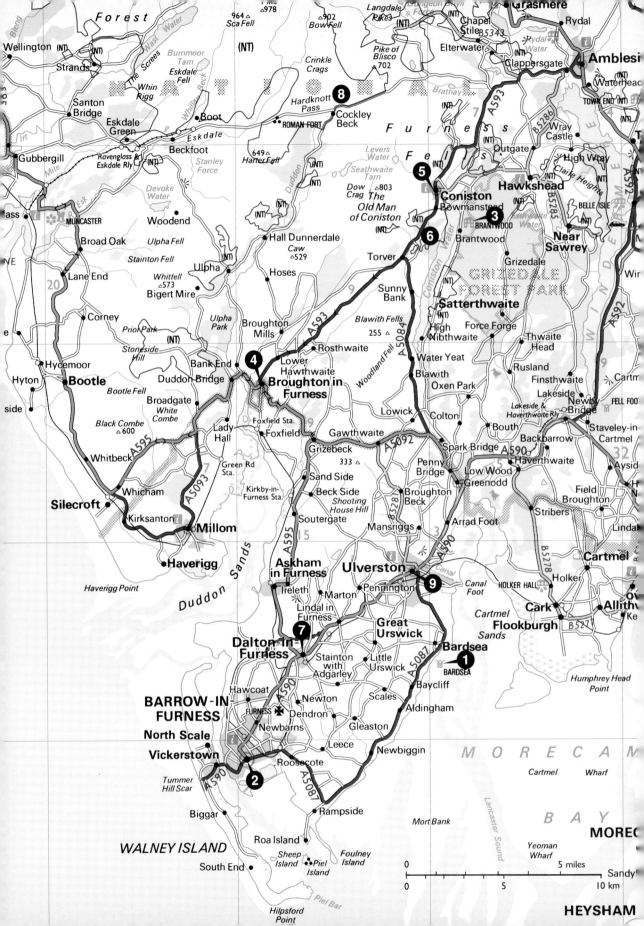

❶ BARDSEA

Sea Wood has large woodland areas with wonderful views over Morecambe Bay. (Open at all times &) There's another fine viewpoint just west of the park, at Birkrigg Common. Margaret Fox, the mother of Quakerism, is buried here, in Sunbrick Burial Ground. Nearby is the Gothic Conishead Priory (1821), now a Tibetan Buddhist centre. The woodland trail across priory land gives some idea of the beauty of this 70 acre estate. Coffee shop. (House open Easter–Sept, Sat–Sun and Bank Hols. Phone 01229 584029) About 3 miles (5 km) south-west of the priory is Gleaston's working water-mill, which has craft workshops and a restaurant. (Open Easter–Sept, Tues–Sun. Phone 01229 869244)

❷ BARROW-IN-FURNESS

North of the town are the red sandstone remains of Furness Abbey, founded in 1127. (Museum and ruins open Easter–Oct daily; Nov–Easter, Wed–Sun) South of Barrow is Piel Castle, a 14th-century defensive tower. A ferry runs from here to Roa Island which, together with Foulney and Walney, is famous for its wildlife. There's a nature trail at Westfield, north of Roa. One of Europe's largest gulleries is on the other side of Walney Channel. (South Walney Gullery and Nature Reserve open Tues–Sun and Bank Hols) ☎ 01229 870156

❸ BRANTWOOD

There's lots for the visitor to see here. Inside the house is a video film of John Ruskin's life and an exhibition of his paintings and some personal possessions. There's also a room devoted to Alfred Wainwright, a tearoom, craft gallery and bookshop. Outside there's a nature trail, a garden and a pier for the steam yacht *Gondola*. (Open mid Mar–mid Nov daily. Rest of the year, Wed–Sun & 015394 41396)

❹ BROUGHTON-IN-FURNESS

The square in this small, friendly 18th-century market town has an obelisk at its centre and fish slabs and stocks nearby.

❺ CONISTON

This dour village used to be famous for its copper, which was mined on the lower slopes of the 2600 ft (790 m) Old Man of Coniston. Nine hundred miners worked here in the 19th century. The National Trust owns the 17th-century Old Hall, which it hopes to open to the public soon. In the churchyard is a Celtic cross memorial to John Ruskin. The Ruskin Museum (Yewdale Road) covers local history, including the story of the world speed record attempts on Coniston Water. (Open Easter–Oct daily) ☎ 015394 41533

❻ CONISTON WATER

The Campbells' association with Coniston Water began in 1939, when the first *Bluebird* power-boat, driven by Malcolm Campbell, set a new world speed record of 141.74 mph (226.8 km/h), but unfortunately ended tragically on 4 January 1967 with Donald Campbell's fatal crash in *Bluebird* during another record attempt. These days a totally different kind of vessel plies the waters, the steam yacht *Gondola* (1859). You can now glide across the lake in fully restored Victorian splendour, thanks to the National Trust. (Regular sailings Apr–early Nov. Pier at Coniston. Phone 015394 41288) Alternatively, you can paddle your own canoe or captain your own rowing boat, sailing dinghy or motor boat by hiring one from the National Park's boating centre at Coniston.

❼ DALTON-IN-FURNESS

The castle here is really only a tower, built in the 1300s by the monks of Furness Abbey. (Open Apr–late Sept, Sat afternoons only. Phone 01229 463330 for key) George Romney (1734–1802), the famous portrait painter, was born in the town and, after a lifetime spent away from it, is buried here. South Lakes Wild Animal Park is at Crossgate, Dalton. Phone 01229 466086.

❽ HARDKNOTT AND WRYNOSE PASSES

With 1 in 3 gradients en route and sheer drops off route, these two passes are not for the faint-hearted. To make matters worse, the road can get very crowded in summer. At the summit of Wrynose Pass (1281 ft/391 m) you'll find the Three Shires Stone to mark the point where, until 1974, Lancashire, Westmorland and Cumberland met. Now, whichever way you turn, it's Cumbria. Hardknott rises higher than Wrynose, to 1291 feet (394 m). Near the top is the Roman fort of Mediobogdum, built c. AD 130 to house a garrison of 500 or so infantry. The walls, with corner towers and gates on each side, are still standing, as are the foundations of the HQ, the granary, the commander's house and the bath house. (Open all year daily)

❾ ULVERSTON

The landmark at Ulverston is a 100 foot (30.5 m) tall 'lighthouse' on top of Hoad Hill, a memorial to local lad Sir John Barrow (1764–1848), who was secretary to the Admiralty for 40 years. (Open June and summer Sundays and Bank Hols, or when the red flag is flying) The town has a wide variety of attractions. Furness Galleries (Theatre Street) is renowned for dolls' houses and furniture hand-made on the premises, and also houses an exhibition area. (Open Tues–Sat. Phone 01229 587657 &) Cumbria Crystal (Lightburn Road) has demonstrations of full-lead crystal being blown, cut and polished. (Open Mon–Fri &) The Laurel and Hardy Museum (Stan Laurel was born here in 1890) in Upper Brook Street has mementoes, photographs and showings of films of the great comic duo. (Open daily)

Just outside Ulverston, on the Barrow road, stands Swarthmoor Hall (1586), the first Quaker centre, and the home of Judge Thomas Fell and his wife Margaret in the 17th century. They be-friended George Fox, the leader of the Quakers, from 1652 onwards. Eleven years after Judge Fell's death, in 1658, Fox and Margaret married. Today the house is still owned by the Society of Friends and is open to visitors. (May be closed in 1996 for refurbishment. Phone 01229 583204) ☎ 01229 587120

Sheep-Farming in Lakeland

The four-hourly feed (EJF)

Tending ewes in winter, Kirkstone Pass (EJF)

Farmer shearing with hand clippers (EJF)

Inspecting tups at market (EJF)

Herdwick tups (EJF)

66   *Preceding page:* Gathering sheep at Watendlath (EJF)

Yan, Tyan, Tethera, Methera, Pimp, Sethera, Lethera, Hovera, Dovera, Dick – your eyelids should be drooping by now because you've been counting sheep Borrowdale style; Yan is one and Dick is ten.

Cumbria is home to 10 per cent of the sheep in England. The commonest breed in Lakeland nowadays is the dark-faced, grey-muzzled Swaledale, which has several advantages over the most traditional breed, the thick set, white-faced Herdwick. Swaledales breed younger, produce better quality wool and have more milk. Herdwicks produce more wool but of a rougher texture;

Returning ewes to the fell, Langdale

theirs is generally used for carpets whereas the soft Swaledale wool is of the right quality for sweaters. Herdwicks are tougher customers all round, able to withstand harsh conditions – such as surviving for two weeks in a snowdrift – and nimble enough to jump over a 4 ft (1.2 m) wall. Sheep-farmers admire the physical prowess of the hardy Herdwick but prefer the economic edge of the Swaledale.

The sheep-farmer's year typically begins in November when the tups (or rams) are run with the ewes on the better land lower down. A tup is expected to service about 60 ewes and gets extra feed for extra work (hence the expression 'getting your oats'). The ewes are then moved to higher land, ideally onto the fellside. It's vital that the ewes have been well fed before they are moved. They can lose up to 20 per cent of their bodyweight and an undernourished ewe may even re-absorb her foetus in an attempt to make up the nutritional shortfall. The farmer gives his ewes extra feed during the last weeks of pregnancy to help them though this vital period.

In April the ewes are gradually rounded up on the high ground. Fell dogs (sheepdogs that can work alone and a long way from the shepherd) are used for this task. Lambing takes place on the lower ground. A different kind of sheepdog is needed to herd the ewes at this time. The dogs mustn't bark or frighten the nervous animals but do their job quietly and unobtrusively. Ideally, lambing will be completed in May and the flock taken back to the fellside. This allows the farmer to get a crop of hay for feed from his lower land. The sheep are brought back down again in July for shearing and dipping, and then it's back up again to the higher land until October when the sheep sales start. Young males and 4- or 5-year-old Swaledale ewes may be sold to farms in the lowlands, the males for fattening for meat and the ewes for interbreeding with lowland rams. The ewes and rams that are kept back by the sheep-farmers will begin the process all over again come November.

Sheep-farming in Lakeland is a hard way of earning a living. The land in the region is generally low grade and, on the fells, it's winter for ten months of the year. Farmers receive very little for the wool and the subsidies for stock and grants for improvements, on which they rely, are decreasing. The drop in the value of agricultural land and stock is a stark reflection of the problems they face. And yet although many of these farmers live on the economic margin, they are in many ways at the centre of the constant struggle to keep Lakeland looking its best. It is they who perform the tricky and time-consuming task of maintaining the traditional drystone walls, and who discourage the relentless march of that poisonous weed bracken, which advances at the rate of one yard (one metre) per year over the best soil unless checked.

There are several sheep events held annually in Lakeland. The most popular are the Wasdale Show in October and the sheepdog trials at Rydal and Patterdale in August.

West Windermere

Wooden sculpture, Grizedale Forest Park

A corner of Hawkshead

Elterwater

Hill Top Farm, near Sawrey

Stott Park Bobbin Mill

The Hawkshead area is like a self-contained island, flanked by Coniston Water to the west and Windermere to the east. It's topped by the volcanic crags and waterfalls around Elterwater in the north, and it's tailed by the River Leven's estuary in the south. Almost all the region's rock is of the soft, sedimentary, south Lakeland type, which gives broad valleys, low hills and gentle slopes. This means there's more farm-land, hamlets and villages than natural dramatic features, but it's a very beautiful area nonetheless.

The area's woodland was also one of its economic mainstays; there are records of the industry dating back to 1430 and only eventually fading out about 100 years ago. The woodland industry here was called coppicing. Each tree trunk was cut down so as to produce long thin poles from the shoots. The process gave about 15 poles per tree every 15 years. Many of the poles

Hawkshead Grammar School

were made into charcoal locally on circular platforms called pitsteads. The charcoal was then used to fire the bloomeries that made iron. (Bloomery sites are easy to find – just look for the slag heaps.) More sophisticated blast furnaces were eventually introduced but charcoal held its place in the iron industry for a very long time; at Ealing Hearth near Backbarrow they were still using it in 1936.

The charcoal had other uses. It's a basic ingredient of gunpowder, so this too was made in the district. Naturally, such factories were built in isolated areas because of the danger of accidents; in 1863 an explosion at the Low Wood factory killed six and was heard as far away as Keswick. Once made, the powder was stored in barrels. About 100 years ago a quarter of a million barrels were needed every year for the gunpowder alone.

Lakeside & Haverthwaite Railway engine

Tarn Hows

In addition to providing the wood for the barrels, the coppiced woodland also supplied the wood for bobbins, the reels then used for winding cotton in factories. One large mill could use ten million bobbins and 10 per cent of these needed replacing every week. Lakeland wood also went into making carts, clogs, pick-axe handles and toggles for Royal Navy duffle coats. Some of the oak poles were split into thin strips and then woven to make swill baskets. The bark of oak trees was also used, to make tannin for tanning leather; half a woods-man's income could come from this alone. It really was a case of 'there's gold to be made out of them thar woods'.

Charcoal burners crop up as 'colliers' in Arthur Ransome's book, *Swallows and Amazons*. Ransome claimed to be the youngest person ever to reach the top of Coniston Old Man – his father had carried him there when he was only a few weeks old, in 1884. The Ransome family generally spent their holidays on or around Coniston Water; Bethecar, near Nibthwaite, was a favourite base. Arthur attended a prep school at Windermere and decided at this time that he wanted to be a writer. Though his own family were opposed to the idea, he persisted and was given great encouragement by the brilliant Collingwoods, the owners of the original *Swallow*. Ransome's writing was inter-

Haverthwaite Station

Grizedale Forest Park

Parachute water tank, Haverthwaite Station

rupted by World War I and the Russian Revolution, the events of which he covered as a reporter. When he eventually managed to get back to the Lakes, in 1925, he bought a house at Low Ludderburn, near Windermere, and settled down to his chosen career. *Swallows and Amazons* was published in 1930. Appropriately, *Esperance* (Captain Flint's houseboat in the book) can be found at the Windermere Steamboat museum today. Ransome had a series of Lakeland homes from 1925 until his death in 1967. His last was Hill Top at Haverthwaite. The writer is buried at Rusland and you can see a replica of his writing room at Kendal.

Beatrix Potter is another famous writer with a strong Lakeland connection. At Hill Top, near Sawrey, you can see the 'new room' where she did much of her work. The whole house is exactly as Beatrix Potter knew it. She bought Hill Top in 1905 with the proceeds from her first book, *The Tale of Peter Rabbit*, which she had originally published herself after seven publishers turned it down. The book had started as a letter to a little boy called Noel, the son of a former governess, in 1893. In the letter Beatrix confided that she hadn't an idea what to write to him about so she'd tell him a story with pictures instead. The inspiration for the story had come to Beatrix many years 73

Tarn Hows

Anne Tyson's cottage, Hawkshead

A village inn

View across Tarn Hows

earlier, in the 1880s when as a girl of 16 she had first visited the Lakes with her parents and stayed at Wray Castle which they had rented for the duration of the holiday. And so began Beatrix's love affair with the region and the stimulus which found expression in her animal characters and their adventures. Beatrix's suffocatingly formal parents did not encourage her to write, and the only support she received was from the local vicar and founder of the National Trust, Hardwicke

Wray Castle

Rawnsley. The purchase of Hill Top was a long-overdue bid for independence. Beatrix wrote 13 books over a period of eight years in the few weeks each year she could snatch away from her demanding parents and spend at the house. During this time she met William Heelis, a local Hawkshead solicitor, who helped her buy Castle Farm in 1909. The couple married in 1913, much to the displeasure of her parents who thought she'd married beneath her. Castle Farm now became Beatrix's main home, with Hill Top kept on as her private museum. From this point on, Beatrix more or less stopped writing and put her energies into new interests. Breeding Herdwick sheep and the conservation of the Lakeland countryside became her passions. When she died in 1943, aged 77, she left 15 farms and over 4000 acres to the National Trust. However, it's because of her books that people visit Hill Top in their droves. There's a special magic in recognizing Tom Kitten's stamping ground or being able to see the very doll's house that 'the two bad mice' wrecked so effectively.

❶ ELTERWATER

The name Elterwater literally means 'swan lake' in Norse. The lake itself is the smallest in Lakeland. To its north is the site of an old gunpowder works, now a time-share property with an excellent sports centre which you can use if you buy a day ticket. (The Langdale Hotel and Country Club is open daily. Phone 015394 37302 ♿)

Also to the north is Fibrecrafts of Barnhowe, a firm specializing in hand-spinning, weaving and dyeing supplies. Half-day courses are held on hand-spinning. (Open Easter–Nov daily; closed Sun afternoon ♿. Phone 015394 37346)

To the south of Elterwater are the villages of Skelwith Bridge and Colwith, noted for their waterfalls.

❷ GRAYTHWAITE HALL GARDENS

This place is a must for flower enthusiasts: 7 acres of rhododendrons, azaleas and flowering shrubs set in grounds landscaped by Thomas Mawson between 1888 and 1890. (Open Apr–Jun daily)

❸ GRIZEDALE FOREST PARK

Here you'll find displays on the forest and its wildlife through the ages. There are computers, a shop, wildlife playground, orienteering trails, seven waymarked walks, hides where you can watch wildlife, and a collection of modern sculpture. (Centre open Apr–Oct and late Dec daily ♿ ♿. Forest and trails open all year. Phone 01229 860373)

❹ HAWKSHEAD

This picturesque village of whitewashed cottages and meandering cobbled streets is very popular. There's a large car park just outside the village. The grammar school (founded in 1588 and housed in a building of 1675) was attended by William Wordsworth between 1779 and 1787. You can see the desk on which he carved his name. (Open Easter–Oct daily) William boarded with Anne Tyson. Her house in the village is marked with a plaque, although it is uncertain whether William lodged at this particular house. The Beatrix Potter Gallery (Main Street) has on display around 150 of the writer's illustrations. It used to be the office of Beatrix's husband, William Heelis, and is virtually unchanged since his time. (Open Apr–early Nov, Sun–Thurs. Phone 015394 36355) There are some lovely views to be had from the church, St Michael's, which dates from Tudor times.

About half a mile north of the village is Hawkshead Courthouse, dating from the 1400s. It was part of Hawkshead Hall and is all that is left of the manorial buildings once owned by the monks of Furness Abbey. (Open Apr–early Nov daily; key obtainable from National Trust shop at Hawkshead) If you head south out of Hawkshead village, you'll come to Esthwaite Water, a private lake. The trout farm on the west side of the lake keeps the waters well stocked for anglers. Rainbow trout grow to almost 13 lb (6 kg). There's an attractive picnic area and boats can be hired at the southern end of the lake. (Open daily ☎ 015394 36525

❺ HILL TOP

This small 17th-century house near Sawrey was the first of several homes owned by Beatrix Potter. While living at Hill Top she wrote many of her best-loved books and introduced characters such as Tom Kitten, Samuel Whiskers and Jemima Puddleduck. Today the house is a museum devoted to every aspect of the life and work of its former owner and is exactly as she knew it, right down to the furniture and china. Hill Top is very popular; so much so that the National Trust has had to stop publicizing it. (Open Apr–early Nov, Mon–Wed and Sat–Sun ♿. Phone 015394 36269) Nearby, close to Far Sawrey, is the ferry landing. From here a 6 mile (9 km) waymarked (with white posts) path leads you up Claife Heights and on to Hawkshead. If the whole route sounds too strenuous, just do the first half-mile – you'll be rewarded with magnificent views.

❻ LAKESIDE AND HAVERTHWAITE RAILWAY

The steam trains of this railway connect with the steamers on Lake Windermere. The trip takes 18 minutes one way. (Trains run daily over Easter then early May–early Oct ♿ ♿. The collection of locomotives at Haverthwaite is open daily. Phone 015395 31594)

Sights en route include: at Lakeside, the Campbell Legend Exhibition on board the lake cruiser *Swift*. This houses replicas of the *Bluebird* car of 1935 and the *Bluebird* hydroplane of 1967. (Open Easter Sun–late Oct daily ♿. Phone 015395 58509); and at Low Wood, near Haverthwaite, the old gunpowder works, now occupied by craftsmen. Art Crystal is housed in the Clock Tower building, where you can see demonstrations of glass-engraving. (Open daily. Phone 015395 31796)

❼ RUSLAND HALL

Built in 1720 with gardens landscaped by 'Capability' Brown. The gardens and house are closed to the public. The writer Arthur Ransome, best-known for *Swallows and Amazons*, is buried in Rusland churchyard.

❽ STOTT PARK BOBBIN MILL

Don't be put off by the rather dull-sounding name. This working factory, built in 1835, is a genuine slice of the past, preserved in all its glory by English Heritage. (Open Apr–Oct daily ♿ ♿. Phone 015395 31087)

❾ TARN HOWS

Lakeland connoisseurs shun this place precisely because it is a great favourite of so many other people. The views are super but you'll have to arrive early to avoid the crush.

❿ WRAY CASTLE

This place, in the village of Low Wray, looks like a Hollywood film set but is, in fact, a Victorian folly (built 1840–7). It used to be the home of a Liverpool surgeon and is now a college for marine engineers. The grounds only are open to the public.

Just south of High Wray is Latterbarrow, an excellent and very accessible viewpoint (803 ft/ 245 m); approach via the footpath from the west.

South-East Lakeland

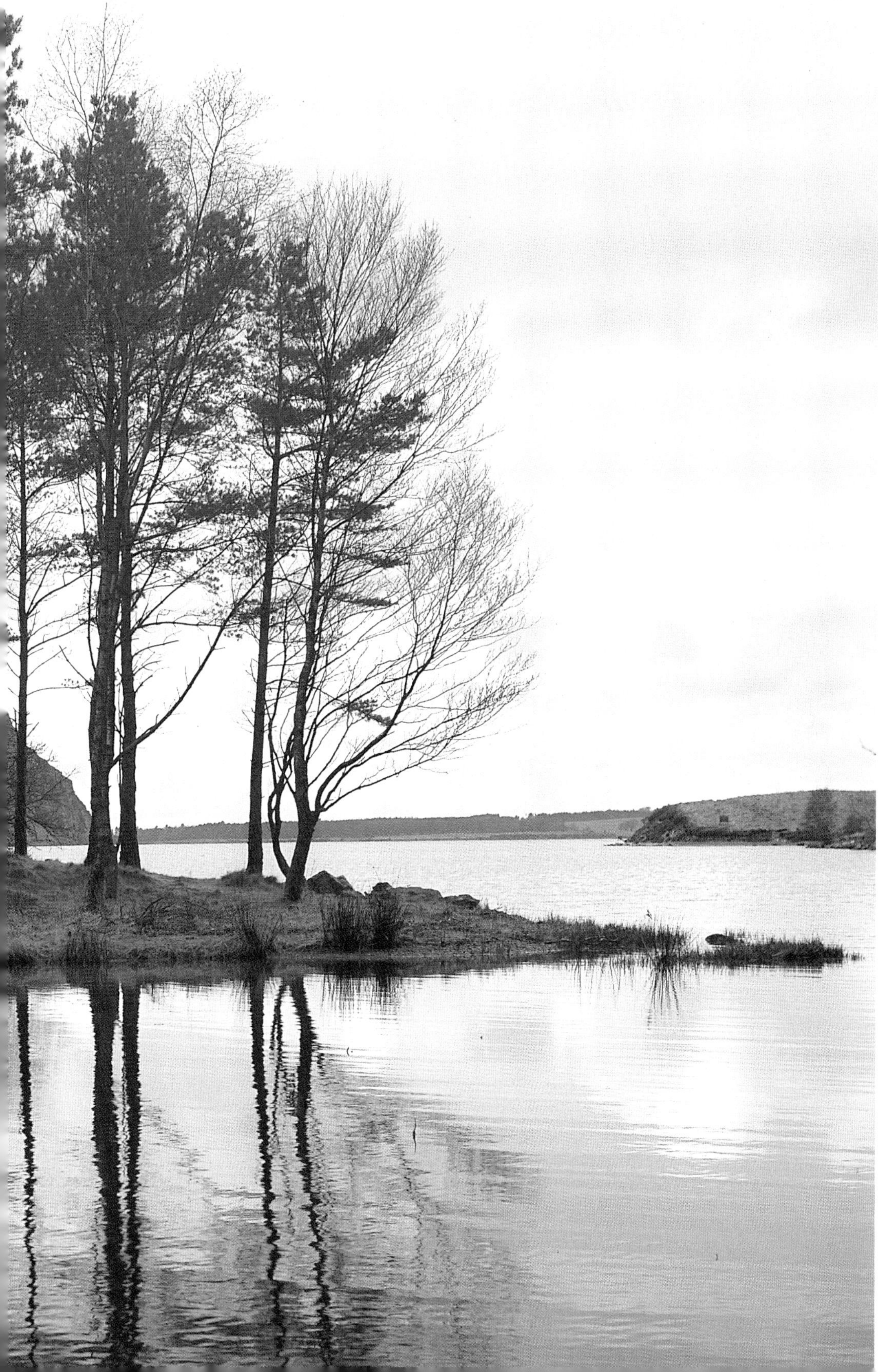

Brockhole National Park Centre

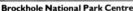

Waterhead, Windermere

The shores of Windermere and the valley of the River Kent become very crowded in summer so you may prefer to explore the hills between the two. The minor roads and small farming settlements lend a quiet and very appealing charm to this south-east corner of Lakeland.

The area is dominated by Kendal, which has many more attractions than any other town in the Lake District. Often called the gateway to the Lakes, Kendal is still involved in manufacturing.

Items ranging from snuff to K's shoes (the K standing for Kendal) are made here. The town is the home of Kendal Mint Cake, a mixture of a little mint essence, some glucose and lots of sugar. This concoction has been carried on many an expedition and has even been eaten on top of Mount Everest.

Kendal has been famous for its cloth for many centuries; the town's motto, *Pannus mihi Panis*, ('cloth is my bread') reflects this. In the Middle

Lake Windermere

The Mason's Arms, Cartmel Fell

Ages there was a type of cloth called Kendal Green which was heavy, warm, waterproof and often dyed green, hence the name. In Shakespeare's plays, Kendal Green seems either to have been worn almost exclusively by 'knaves' or it turns up in 'threadbare' condition. Luxury cloth was also made in Kendal. In 1543 King Henry VIII was so impressed by the gift of a coat of Kendal cloth that he ordered another and started a fashion for it at court. The present was given by local resident Catherine Parr, who was born at Kendal Castle in 1512. Later she became his sixth wife and fortunately managed to bury him before he could either divorce or execute her. Henry was her third husband. Catherine married her love, Sir Thomas Seymour, in 1547 but sadly died a year later shortly after giving birth to their first child. The town proudly preserves Catherine's own tiny, handwritten prayerbook; it's only $2\frac{1}{3}$ in $\times$ $1\frac{1}{2}$ in (6 cm $\times$ 4 cm). If you'd like to see it, enquire at the

Holy Trinity parish church, Kendal

River Kent, Kendal

Kendal

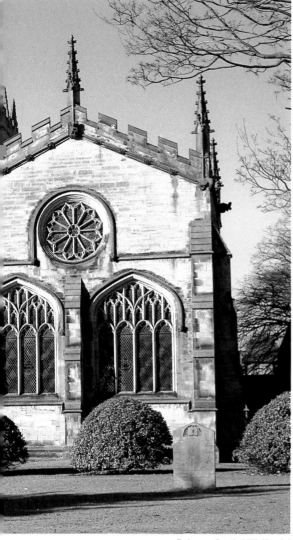

Ruins on Castle Hill, Kendal

Tourist Information Centre in The Town Hall, where it's kept.

The region produces both dairy cattle (generally Friesians) and beef cattle (mainly Friesian cows crossed with foreign bulls such as Simmentals or Limousins). The advantage of cattle is that they help improve hill land by eating coarse grass that sheep won't touch. The disadvantages are that they put on less weight in comparison to sheep – particularly on poorer grass – and need a good supply of feed in winter when they're housed. In 1986 sheep outnumbered cattle by nearly 9:1 in

Waterside, Kendal

the National Park, although cattle remain a vital part of the farming industry.

Just 2 miles (3 km) south of Kendal is a railway junction called Oxenholme. From here a single line branches off the Euston–Glasgow mainline and potters gently on through the countryside via Kendal and Staveley to Windermere. It's difficult to credit that this humble little track used to carry the Lakes Express, a superb train connecting London with Lakeland. The nondescript two-carriage diesel units nowadays used by British Rail on this line look out of place in the 100 yard (100 m) long platforms built at Windermere to accommodate the Express. When the idea of building the line was first mooted, Wordsworth was one of the many people in the area who bitterly opposed it. His main objection was that it would allow hordes of 'uneducated people' into *his* countryside. These philistines wouldn't appreciate what they saw and would only ruin it for the minority who could

Newby Bridge

Ennerdale Water

appreciate it. Despite a thunderous sonnet published in the *Morning Post* (beginning: 'Is there no nook of English ground secure from rash assault?'), Wordsworth lost. The line was built but stopped three-quarters of a mile (1.2 km) short of the lakeside so as not to disturb the 'quality' dwelling in their villas. Later attempts to extend the line were quashed by the two R's – Rawnsley and Ruskin, representing the great and the good of Victorian England. (Trains run frequently on weekdays. Journey duration is about 25 minutes.)

Wordsworth also hated the indiscriminate planting of larch trees and the selfish positioning of brand new whitewashed houses just where they did maximum damage to the views. In many ways he's one of the early conservationists. In his *Guide to the Lakes* (a best-seller which, ironically, did much to encourage yet more visitors to flock to *his*

Shop sign, Backbarrow, Newby Bridge

Lakeland) Wordsworth came up with the idea that there ought to be some control system to stop the region being ruined. He went on to describe the district as 'a sort of national property, in which every man has a right and interest who has an eye to perceive and a heart to enjoy'. Nothing came of this idea until 1951 when the Lake District National Park, embracing 880 square miles (2279 sq km), was established. (By contrast, in the United States Yellowstone National Park was set up in 1876.)

Land ownership didn't change as a result of the creation of the National Park, but it did mean that special planning restrictions were introduced. A special body (called the Lake District Special Planning Board or the National Park Authority) was also set up to protect the region, keep it beautiful and help the public appreciate it.

85

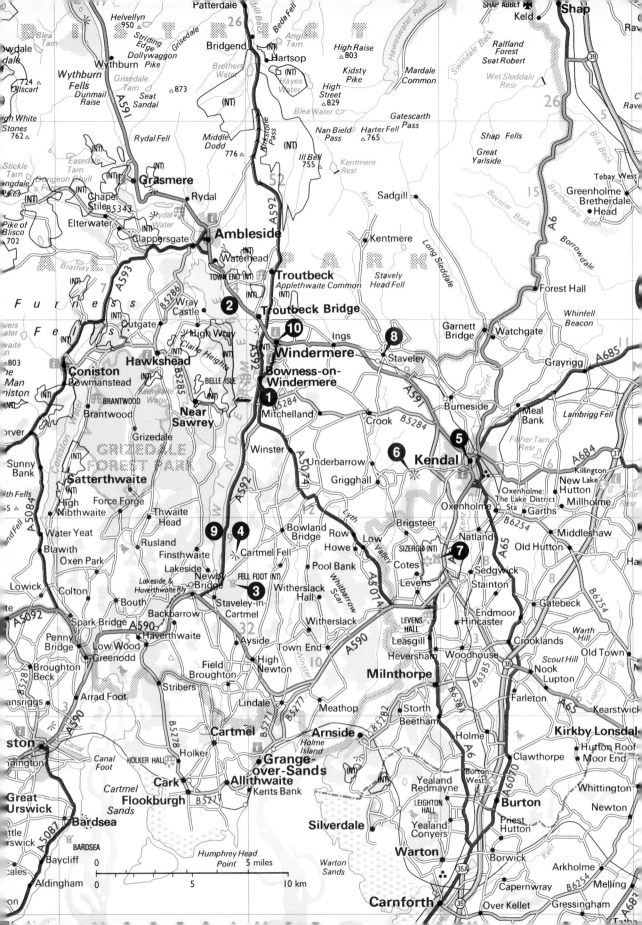

❶ BOWNESS

The attractions of this lakeside town are appropriately watery. The Windermere Steamboat Museum (Rayrigg Road) has two record-breakers on display: *Dolly* (c. 1850), the oldest mechanically-powered boat in the world; and *Esperance* (1869), the oldest boat on Lloyd's Register. Beatrix Potter's rowing boat is here, as is an elegant launch called *Branksome*, which has a tea urn that can boil a gallon of water in ten seconds! The museum also operates steamboat cruises on the lake. (Open Easter–Oct daily ♿ ⛵. Phone 015394 45565) The World of Beatrix Potter on Craig Brow is a celebra-tion of the animal characters created by this famous children's author. (Open daily) ☎ 015394 42895

❷ BROCKHOLE

This is the National Park Centre. It bills itself as 'the Key to the Lakes' and aims to give the new visitor a thorough introduction to the area. There's an exhibition on Lakeland life through the centuries and a superb audiovisual programme. The programme of special activities can range from dog obedience classes through open-air theatre to Household Cavalry displays. In the grounds (landscaped by Thomas Mawson) you'll find well-tended flowerbeds, putting and croquet lawns, and an adventure playground. There are also orienteering and nature trails to follow. Restaurant. (Open late Mar–Nov daily ♿ ⛵. Phone 015394 46601)

❸ FELL FOOT PARK

All that remains of the Georgian house that used to stand here are its outbuildings. These have been converted by the National Trust into a shop, information centre and café. The 18 acres (7.3 hectares) of land on the lakeshore also belong to the trust. The place is worth visiting for the views alone. There are also fishing, bathing and picnic areas, and rowing boats for hire. (Park open all year daily. Amenities open Easter–end Oct daily ♿ ⛵. Phone 015395 31273)

❹ GUMMERS HOWE

This superb viewpoint (1054 ft/ 324 m) is reached after a half-mile walk from the car park on the unclassified road leading from the Fell Foot area.

❺ KENDAL

Once the county town of Westmorland, Kendal has a lot to offer, including a very large and fine parish church, the remains of two castles (both open at any time) and Castle Dairy (Wildman Street), parts of which date back to the 1300s. (Open Easter–Sept, Weds afternoons only) There are several museums here. Abbot Hall (Kirkland) is a Georgian house containing antique porcelain, glass, silver, furniture and paintings, as well as a fine collection of modern art. Part of the Abbot Hall complex houses the Museum of Lakeland Life, which vividly illustrates everyday life in the area with replicas of a Victorian street, farmhouse rooms, workshops and Arthur Ransome's study. Kendal Museum (Station Road) specializes in local history (including natural history) and has a display devoted to fell walker Arthur Wainwright. (All three museums are open daily, except Jan ♿. Phone 01539 722464) Kendal also has the lively Brewery Arts Centre (Highgate), with a restaurant. (Open daily ♿) You can see Axminster carpets being made at Goodacre Carpets (Aynam Road). (Open mid Apr–mid Oct, Wed and Fri afternoons ♿) Kendal usually hosts the Westmorland County Show in early September. The Kendal Gathering is a festival that starts on August Bank Holiday weekend and ends three weeks later. The torchlight procession is one of the highlights of the festival and is very popular. ☎ 01539 725758

❻ SCOUT SCAR

This viewpoint (813 ft/250 m) is easily reached from the car park in the quarry midway between Kendal and Underbarrow.

❼ SIZERGH CASTLE

The Strickland family have lived here for over 700 years. The pele tower (1340) is the largest in Cumbria. There's fine furniture and porcelain inside the house, including what are reputed to be the finest early-Elizabethan wood-carvings in England. Outside is the largest limestone rock garden owned by the National Trust, as well as rose, water and Dutch gardens. (Open Apr–Oct, Sun–Thurs ♿. Phone 015395 60070)

❽ STAVELEY

Formerly a centre of woodland industry, the village has as one of its main features the firm of Peter Hall & Son, specialists in cabinet-making, antique furniture restoring, wood-turning and traditional upholstering. You can watch the craftsmen at work and buy the result. (Open Mon–Sat ♿. Phone 0539 821633)

❾ WINDERMERE

This is the largest lake in England, at 10½ miles (17 km) long and about a mile wide at its broadest point. On Windermere's largest island (just opposite Bowness) is the first round house built in England. Belle Isle House, built in 1774, was the home of the Curwens from 1781. (Not open) There are three ways to cross the lake. A car ferry sails from Bowness Nab to Far Sawrey about every 20 minutes. (Runs every day except Christmas and Boxing days.) The Bowness Bay Boating Company operates passenger services between Bowness and Ambleside; some ferries stop at Brockhole in the summer, while others do a circular cruise. (Open daily except Christmas Day. One launch is wheelchair accessible.) The Windermere Iron Steamboat Company, based at Newby Bridge, sails between Lakeside, Bowness and Ambleside; the full one-way trip takes about 1 hour 20 minutes. (Runs Good Friday–early Nov ♿. Phone 015395 31188)

❿ WINDERMERE TOWN

Windermere is really an expanded hamlet called Birthwaite and is situated one mile from the lake. There are shops and hotels. Just opposite the railway station, which opened in 1847, is a footpath that winds up to the top of Orrest Head (784 ft/239 m), a great viewpoint. ☎ 015394 46499

DANGER
BEWARE
FAST RISING TIDES
QUICKSANDS
HIDDEN CHANNELS
REN WARNS OF INCOMING TIDE
ERGENCY PHONE 999 AND ASK FOR COASTGUARD

The Southern Approaches

Heron Corn Mill, Beetham

View from Duke's bedroom, Holker Hall   Salt marsh near Flookburgh

Flat fish-shaped weathervane on Flookburgh church

Preceding page: View across
90   Morecambe Bay, Grange-over-Sands

The Duke's bedroom, Holker Hall

Cartmel

With no lakes and much of it outside the boundary of the National Park, this area may not seem like Lakeland at all. It is very different from the other areas, with estuaries and a coastline instead of rugged landscape. But it has just as much to offer in the way of great houses, gardens and viewpoints.

The main gateway to southern Lakeland in the past was across the sands of the estuaries of the rivers Kent and Leven at low tide. The sands shift and there are large areas of quicksand, making any crossing a risky venture even when a route has been established. The routes across the sands date back to the time of the Romans and have been used regularly by locals over the centuries. The monks of Conishead Priory, near Ulverston, built an oratory halfway across the Leven estuary in the hope that prayers said for safe journeys would be answered. Earthly assistance was provided in the form of a primitive lighthouse constantly tended by a monk; the ruins of this building can be seen on the island. The monks of Cartmel Priory appointed local guides to take travellers across the Kent estuary. Since the 16th century, when the Priory was dissolved, the Duchy of Lancaster (ie, the Crown) has made the appointments. There was even a stagecoach route across the sands, with regular departures three days a week from Ulverston. Wordsworth could see this procession from his vantage point on Chapel Island, and in 1794 recorded his impressions:

'. . . . . . . .variegated crowd
Of vehicles and travellers, horse and foot,
Wading beneath the conduct of their guide. . .'

This traffic was halted by the advent of the railway in the 1850s which offered a much quicker, more convenient and less dangerous method of crossing the sands. At Grange the tidal bore comes in at 7 mph (15.6 km/h) and has claimed around 140 victims over the years. In 1821 a whole stagecoach disappeared without trace. It's said that the locals would throw dice for the belongings of any traveller who was seen setting off across the sands without a guide. One hopes this doesn't happen today, but to be sure of avoiding an outside chance of becoming an object of barter, hire a guide to take you across.

The region has a high concentration of pele towers. Those at Arnside, Hazelslack, Beetham, Dallam, Heversham, Levens and Sizergh are in very close proximity. Pele towers were built in the

View across to Arnside and its viaduct

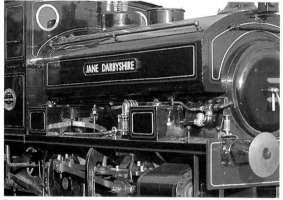

Four views of Carnforth Steam Railway Centre

early 1300s when the English began to lose their iron grip on the Scots, who decided it was about time they got their own back. And so began a turbulent period for this prosperous area, which became a constant target of the marauding Scots. Robert the Bruce and his army paid a particularly destructive visit in 1322, rampaging down the east coast and across to Kendal before heading back northwards via Penrith.

Wilkinson monument, Lindale

The pele tower was essentially a bolt-hole that you escaped into when a raid was imminent. It was really pot-luck whether the raiders considered your tower worth the effort of a siege. Most pele towers had three storeys, no windows on the ground floor (where animals were stabled) and one low, narrow entry door reinforced with iron. The ceilings were of stone. The spiral staircase leading up to the top of the tower was narrow and easy to defend if the main door was breached. Most of the defending was done from the battlements at the top of the tower and through 'murder holes', exit points for all sorts of unspeakable missiles destined for the forces below. The pele towers were well used until the Scots were defeated in the Tudor period, finally becoming redundant in 1603 with the accession of James I to the thrones of England and Scotland.

93

❶ ARNSIDE

This town stands on the estuary of the River Kent. A railway line runs across the estuary, over a 50-pier viaduct, and offers a leisurely way of seeing coastal Lakeland. Just south of the town, a nature trail leads up to the viewpoint of Arnside Knott (521 ft/159 m).

❷ CARTMEL

This very attractive village is dominated by its church, the remains of a priory founded in 1188, which is one of the finest medieval buildings in Lakeland. (Open daily &) The gatehouse of the priory (c. 1330) was used as the local grammar school (1624–1790) and is now let by the National Trust as an art gallery and studio. (Open daily. Phone 015395 36602) Cartmel has England's smallest National Hunt race course. (Meetings held on spring and late summer Bank Hols) and a large agricultural show held annually in early August.

❸ DOCKER PARK FARM

This working farm with horses, pigs, sheep, goats and poultry also holds exhibitions and demonstrations, and has an indoor play area. (Open Easter–Oct daily & ⚞. Phone 015242 21331)

❹ FLOOKBURGH

The main trade of this town is fish, especially the flat fish called fluke (hence the name). Even the weathervane on the local church is in the shape of a flat fish. The Cumbria Steam Gathering is held here in late July.

❺ GRANGE-OVER-SANDS

The climate here is so mild that exotic plants such as yuccas feel quite at home. 'Cumbria's Riviera', as Grange calls itself, has a mile-long (1.6 km) promenade and ornamental municipal gardens. The sands, after which the town gets its name, have always been treacherous and today there is still an official guide to help those people who want to cross them. Above the town, at the top of Hampsfell (727 ft/222 m), there's a small shelter for travellers. The views from here are wonderful. ☎ 015395 34026

❻ HERON CORN MILL

Milling has gone on at Beetham since 1220. The present water-powered mill is still in full working order. There's a picnic area here and also a museum of paper-making. (Open Easter–Sept, Tues–Sun and Bank Hols. Phone 015395 63363)

❿❷ HALECAT GARDEN NURSERY

This nursery near Witherslack has a small but beautiful garden created around a mid 19th-century house. Fine views over Morecambe Bay. (Open Mon–Fri and also Sun during summer. Phone 015395 52229)

❽ HOLKER HALL

The Cavendish family (a branch of the Duke of Devonshire's line) still owns this house, which was largely rebuilt in 1874. Inside, you'll find the usual fine pictures and furniture but with the bonus of fresh flowers in every room and rope barriers in none of them. There are 25 acres (10 hectares) of gardens, a display of Victorian, Edwardian and wartime kitchens and an adventure playground, together with a photographic display and shop. The Lakeland Motor Museum (separate admission) is within the complex of Holker Hall and has over 80 historic cars and a replica garage of the 1920s on display. The hall hosts the Great Garden and Countryside Festival in early June. (Both Hall and Motor Museum open Apr–Oct, Mon–Fri and Sun & ⚞. Phone 015395 58509)

❾ LEIGHTON HALL

The present hall, built in the late 18th century, belongs to the Gillow family of furniture-makers. The house is full of examples of their wares. Trained birds of prey, including eagles, are flown in the gardens. (Open May–Sept, Tues–Fri and Sun &. Phone 01524 734474) North-west of here, between Silverdale and Yealand Conyers, is Leighton Moss, a 300 acre (121 hectare) RSPB reserve set among meres, reeds and willows. The visitor centre has a shop, video, tearoom and display area. (Open daily; facilities closed Tues. Phone 01524 701601) The More-

cambe Bay Bird Sanctuary nearby (just off the Warton to Silverdale road) is an excellent spot for seeing flocks of waders in winter. (No facilities)

❿ LEVENS HALL

This great Elizabethan house was built round a 13th-century pele tower. It's most noted for its gardens (laid out in 1692), especially the topiary, but there's plenty else besides, including an adventure playground and a collection of working steam engines (also steam traction engine afternoons). The house contains some fine pieces of furniture, paintings and, if you're very sharp-eyed, ghosts. The dining room walls are lined with Cordova leather, and there is some exquisite plasterwork. (Open Apr–Sept, Sun–Thurs ⚞. Phone 015395 60321)

⓫ LINDALE

The most important feature in this village is a 40 foot (12 m) cast-iron obelisk standing on the B road to Grange. It was ordered by John Wilkinson (1728–1808) as part of his funeral arrangements, which also included a cast-iron coffin. Wilkinson had helped cast the first iron bridge and had launched the first iron ship. 'Iron Mad' John, as he was called, was originally buried in his garden at Castle Head, just outside the village, with the obelisk erected over his grave. Later his coffin was removed to the local churchyard and the obelisk re-erected at its present site.

⓬ STEAMTOWN RAILWAY CENTRE

Situated at Carnforth, Steamtown has around 30 diesel and steam engines ranging in size from a giant express to a tiny tank engine. You can also see coaches, a signal box, a coaling plant and miniature and model railways. (Open Easter–Oct daily. Minimal facilities in winter. Phone 01524 732100 for details of when the engines or the miniature railway are working) Next door is Carnforth railway station where David Lean's classic 'weepie' *Brief Encounter*, with Trevor Howard and Celia Johnson, was filmed.

The Southern Approaches

Page numbers in italics indicate a gazetteer entry

100 Great Indian Recipes

© Roli & Janssen BV 2010

Published in India by Roli Books
in arrangement with Roli & Janssen BV,
The Netherlands
M-75, Greater Kailash-II Market,
New Delhi 110 048, India.
Phone: ++91-11-40682000.
Fax: ++91-11-29217185
Email: info@rolibooks.com.
Website: rolibooks.com

ISBN: 978-81-7436-764-8

Editor: Neeta Datta
Design: Supriya Saran
Pre press: Jyoti Dey

Printed and bound in China

The publisher is grateful to India Tourism
Development Corporation for providing
the recipes on pages: 10, 13, 14, 16, 19, 22,
24, 29, 32, 39, 43, 46, 48, 52, 55, 56, 58, 67
(top), 68 (top), 72, 75, 81, 84, 93, 96 (top),
98, 101, 104, 106, 109, 114, 122, 127, 132,
135, 136, 139 (bottom), 140, 142

Photographs

Deepak Budhraja: pages 2, 3, 6, 8, 15, 17,
20, 23, 25, 28, 33, 38, 42, 47, 49, 50, 53, 54,
56, 59, 66, 69, 70, 72, 74, 80, 85, 88, 92, 97,
99, 100, 105, 107, 108, 115, 116, 123, 126,
133, 137, 138, 140, 143

Corbis: pages 4-5 and Back cover

Roli Collection: All other photographs and
recipes

100 Great Indian Recipes

Compiled by
MASTER CHEFS OF INDIA

Lustre Press
Roli Books

Contents

Basic Recipes

Brown onion paste

Fry sliced onions on medium heat till brown. Drain the excess oil and allow to cool. Process until pulped (using very little water, if required). Refrigerate in an airtight container.

Coconut milk

Grate 1 coconut and press through a muslin cloth to obtain the first (thick) extract. Boil the grated coconut with equal quantity of water to obtain the second (thin) extract.

If refrigerated, this can stay for up to 3-4 days.

Chicken stock

Take 1 kg chicken, 2 medium-sized onions, chopped, 1 large tomato, chopped, 4 cups / 1 lt / 32 fl oz water, 2 tsp / 8 gm salt, a pinch of turmeric (*haldi*) powder, 1″ piece ginger (*adrak*), chopped, 1 tbsp / 6 gm coriander (*dhaniya*) seeds, 1 cinnamon (*dalchini*), 1″ stick, 4 cloves (*laung*), and 10 black peppercorns (*sabut kali mirch*).

Put the first 6 ingredients into a large pan. Tie the ginger and spices in a muslin cloth and add to the pan. Bring the mixture to the boil, lower heat and simmer for at least 1 hour. Skim off any scum.

Squeeze the muslin bag to extract the flavours. Strain the stock. Remove the meat from the bones and keep aside. Refrigerate stock when cool and skim off any excess congealed fat, if desired.

Add 1 sautéed onion, 1 tomato, cooked meat, and some uncooked pasta / rice for a nutritious soup.

Vegetable stock

Combine 4 carrots (*gajar*), washed and scrubbed; 8 whole spring onions (*hara pyaz*); 6 outer lettuce leaves, 1 tsp salt, and 4 cups / 1 lt / 32 fl oz water together. Bring the mixture to the boil. Cover, lower heat and simmer for 30 minutes. Strain the stock through a muslin cloth and use as required.

Mint (*Pudina*) chutney

Take 4 cups / 100 gm / 3½ oz Mint (*pudina*) leaves, chopped, 4 cups / 100 gm / 3½ oz Green coriander (*hara dhaniya*), 2 tbsp / 24 gm Onions, chopped, 1 tbsp / 24 gm Ginger (*adrak*), chopped, 4-5 Green chillies, chopped, ½ cup / 100 gm / 3½ oz Yoghurt (*dahi*), 1 tsp / 2 gm Mango powder (*amchur*), 1 tbsp / 20 gm Sugar, Salt to taste and 1 tsp / 4 gm Black salt (*kala namak*).

Blend the mint leaves, green coriander, onions, ginger, and green chillies to make a smooth paste. Keep aside In a mixing bowl. Whisk yoghurt with mango powder, sugar, salt, and black salt. Add the mint paste and mix well. Serve with kebabs.

Soft cottage cheese (*chenna*)

For about 400 gm / 14 oz; boil 2 lt / 64 fl oz milk in a deep pot and remove from heat. Add 160 ml / 5 fl oz vinegar or lemon juice till the milk curdles. Transfer the curdled milk into a muslin cloth to drain out the whey. Use either in crumbled form or else wrap in a muslin cloth and press down with a weight for half an hour or so. This will form into a block, which can then be cut to desired size pieces.

Tamarind (*imli*) pulp

Take 200 gm / 7 oz of seedless tamarind. Add 3 cups / 750 ml / 24 fl oz water and boil for 5 minutes. Strain the mixture and use as required.

Wholemilk fudge (*khoya*)

Boil milk in a wok (*kadhai*). Reduce heat and cook, stirring occasionally, till the quantity is reduced to half. Then stir constantly and scrape from all sides till a thick paste-like consistency is obtained. Allow to cool.

Soups & Beverages

Dahi Shorba

Tangy yoghurt soup

Picture facing page top

Ingredients

1½ cups / 300 gm / 11 oz Yoghurt (*dahi*)
5 tbsp / 25 gm Butter
2 tsp / 6 gm Fenugreek seeds (*methi dana*)
2 tsp / 6 gm Mustard seeds (*rai*)
1½ cups / 150 gm / 5 oz Gram flour
    (*besan*)
Salt to taste
1 tsp / 2 gm White pepper (*safed mirch*)
    powder
1 tsp / 2 gm Turmeric (*haldi*) powder
1 cup / 225 gm White radish (*mooli*),
    peeled, cut into cubes
12 cups / 3 lt Water
2 tsp / 10 gm Curry leaves (*kadhi patta*)
1 tsp / 2 gm Curry powder
½ cup / 100 ml / 3½ fl oz Cream

Method

Melt the butter in a pot; add fenugreek seeds and mustard seeds. Sauté till they crackle. Add gram flour, salt, white pepper powder, turmeric powder, and radish blended in yoghurt.

Add 4 cups water and cook till a pleasing smell of gram flour emanates. Reduce heat and simmer for 10 minutes.

Add the remaining water and curry leaves, cook on low heat till it comes to the boil. Stir in the curry powder. Remove from heat and pass through a soup strainer.

Stir in the cream, pour into individual soup bowls and serve.

Tamatar ka Shorba

Tangy and spicy tomato soup

Picture facing page bottom

Ingredients

800 gm / 28 oz Tomatoes, chopped
4 tbsp / 60 ml / 2 fl oz Vegetable oil
3-4 Cinnamon (*dalchini*), 1″ sticks
5-6 Cloves (*laung*)
2 Bay leaves (*tej patta*)
4 Green cardamoms (*choti elaichi*)
½ tbsp / 12 gm Ginger (*adrak*), chopped
1 tbsp / 12 gm Garlic (*lasan*), chopped
4 cups / 1 lt / 32 fl oz Water
Salt to taste
Black pepper (*kali mirch*) powder to taste
3 tbsp / 60 ml / 2 fl oz Cream

Method

Heat the oil in a deep pan; add the whole spices and sauté till they crackle.

Add the tomatoes, ginger, garlic, and water. Bring the mixture to the boil and cook on low heat for 30 minutes.

Remove from heat and mash the tomatoes. Strain the liquid through a soup strainer into another pan. Discard the tomato pulp.

Heat the soup, adjust the seasoning and remove from heat. Stir in the cream and serve hot.

Tamatar Nariyal ka Shorba

Serves: 4
Preparation Time: 15 min
Cooking Time: 30 min

Tomato soup flavoured with coconut   Picture facing page centre

Ingredients

500 gm / 1.1 lb Tomatoes, chopped
½ cup / 50 gm / 1¾ oz Coconut (*nariyal*),
  grated
3 tbsp / 45 ml / 1½ fl oz Coconut oil
2 tsp / 6 gm Garlic (*lasan*), chopped
3½ tbsp / 40 gm / 1¼ oz Onion, chopped
1 tbsp / 24 gm Ginger (*adrak*), crushed
Salt to taste
½ tsp / 1 gm White pepper (*safed mirch*)
  powder
4 Bay leaves (*tej patta*)
6 cups / 1½ lt / 48 fl oz Vegetable stock
  (see p.7)
2 tbsp / 40 ml / 1¼ fl oz Cream

Method

Heat the coconut oil in a pot; sauté garlic and onion for a few seconds.

Add the coconut and stir-fry. Add tomatoes and ginger.

Stir in the salt, white pepper powder, bay leaves, and vegetable stock. Simmer for 15-20 minutes till the tomatoes are cooked and tender. Remove from heat and keep aside to cool.

Blend the mixture, strain through a muslin cloth and reheat. Remove from heat and stir in the cream.

Pour into individual soup bowls and serve immediately.

Palak ka Shorba

Serves: 4
Preparation Time: 20 min
Cooking Time: 30 min

Spinach soup   Picture facing page top

Ingredients

500 gm / 1.1 lb Spinach (*palak*), washed,
  finely chopped
2 tbsp / 40 gm / 1¼ oz Butter
2 tbsp / 20 gm Refined flour (*maida*)
5 tsp / 30 gm / 1 oz Ginger (*adrak*),
  chopped
1 tsp / 3 gm Garlic (*lasan*), chopped
5-6 Black peppercorns (*sabut kali mirch*)
4 Bay leaves (*tej patta*)
Salt to taste
a pinch White pepper (*safed mirch*)
  powder
6 cups / 1½ lt / 48 fl oz Vegetable stock
  (see p.7)

Method

Melt the butter in a pot; add refined flour and cook to a sandy texture.

Add ginger, garlic, and spinach; sauté for a few minutes. Add black peppercorns, bay leaves, salt, white pepper powder, and vegetable stock. Simmer for 15-20 minutes.

Remove the spinach from the stock and blend to a purée. Return the spinach purée to the stock and cook for 5 minutes.

Remove from heat, pour into individual soup bowls and serve hot.

Gajar-Santre ka Shorba

Serves: 4
Preparation Time: 1 hr
Cooking Time: 40 min

Carrots blended with orange juice

Picture page 12 bottom

Ingredients

500 gm / 1.1 lb Carrots (*gajar*), cut
  into small cubes
4 cups / 1 lt / 32 fl oz Orange (*santra*)
  juice
5 tsp / 25 gm Butter
1 cup / 120 gm / 4 oz Onions,
  chopped
Salt to taste
1 tsp / 2 gm White pepper (*safed
  mirch*) powder
1½ tbsp / 30 gm / 1 oz Sugar
½ cup / 100 ml / 3½ fl oz Cream

Method

Melt the butter in a pan; add onions and sauté till transparent. Add the carrots and sauté for a minute. Add the remaining ingredients except cream and cook on low heat till the carrot is tender.

Remove from heat and then strain through a muslin cloth.

Reheat the strained soup and stir in the cream. Remove from heat, pour into individual soup bowls and serve hot.

Cold Cucumber Soup

Serves: 4
Preparation Time: 30 min
Cooking Time: 45 min

Green cucumber blended with cream

Picture facing page

Ingredients

1 kg / 2.2 lb Cucumber (*khira*),
  quartered alongwith peel
5 tsp / 25 gm Butter
1 cup / 120 gm / 4 oz Onions,
  quartered
8 cups / 2 lt / 64 fl oz Vegetable stock
  (see p.7), strained
Salt to taste
½ tsp / 1 gm White pepper (*safed
  mirch*) powder
½ cup / 100 ml / 3½ fl oz Cream,
  whipped

Method

Heat the butter in a pot; add onions and sauté till transparent. Add the cucumber and sauté for a few minutes.

Stir in the vegetable stock, salt to taste, and white pepper powder. Cook covered on low heat for 20-25 minutes till the cucumber is tender. Stir in the cream, remove from heat and allow to cool.

Blend the soup to obtain a purée and strain through a muslin cloth.

Pour into individual soup bowls and refrigerate for 1 hour.

Serve chilled, garnished with cream.

Tarbuj ka Sharbat

Watermelon juice flavoured with mint

Ingredients

4 kg / 8.8 lb Watermelon (*tarbuj*)
1 tsp / 2 gm Mint (*pudina*) leaves,
  chopped
Black salt (*kala namak*) to taste

Method

Cut the flesh of the watermelon into small chunks, discard the rind. Remove all the seeds.

Blend the watermelon chunks with mint leaves.

Strain through a muslin cloth and discard the pulp.

Serve chilled in individual glasses with a dash of black salt.

Bel ka Sharbat

Bael squash

Ingredients

1 Bael (*bel*), large
4 cups / 1 lt / 32 fl oz Water
½ cup / 75 gm / 2½ oz Sugar,
  powdered

Method

Break open the bael and remove the pulp.

Soak the pulp in water and leave overnight.

Dissolve the sugar in the water and add to the bael mixture. Strain the mixture through a muslin cloth. Discard the pulp.

Serve chilled in individual glasses.

Facing page left to right: Tarbuj ka Sharbat, Bel ka Sharbat, Tender Coconut Shikanji

Tender Coconut Shikanji

Ginger blended coconut water and lemon   Picture page 17

Ingredients

4 Green or Tender coconuts (*nariyal*)
1 cup / 150 gm / 5 oz Sugar,
   powdered
3 Lemons (*nimbu*)
2 tsp / 10 ml Ginger (*adrak*) juice,
   strained

Method

Extract the water from the coconuts.

Dissolve the sugar in the coconut water. Add juice of lemons and ginger. Strain through a muslin cloth. Chill in a refrigerator.

Pour into serving glasses and serve.

Salted Lassi

Salted buttermilk   Picture facing page

Ingredients

1 kg / 2.2 lb Yoghurt (*dahi*)
2 cups / 500 ml / 16 fl oz Water
1 tbsp / 9 gm Salt
1 cup Ice cubes

Method

Mix yoghurt with water, salt and ice cubes until thoroughly mixed. Pour into serving glasses.

Serve chilled, as a starter or an accompaniment to a meal.

Chicken

Murg Bannu Kebab

Serves: 4
Preparation Time: 45 min
Cooking Time: 20 min

Egg-coated chicken kebabs

Ingredients

900 gm / 2 lb Chicken, cut into
  boneless cubes, washed, dried
2 tsp / 8 gm Salt
1 tsp / ½ gm Dry fenugreek (*kasoori
  methi*) powder
2 tbsp / 36 gm / 1¼ oz Ginger-garlic
  (*adrak-lasan*) paste
2 tsp Green chillies, chopped
1 tbsp / 4 gm Green coriander (*hara
  dhaniya*), chopped
1 tsp / 5 ml Vinegar (*sirka*)
5 tbsp / 75 ml / 2½ fl oz Vegetable oil
5 tsp / 15 gm Gram flour (*besan*),
  sieved
2½ tbsp / 37 gm /
  1¼ oz Breadcrumbs, fresh
6 Egg yolks, whisked

Method

Mix salt, dry fenugreek powder, ginger-garlic paste, green chillies, green coriander, and vinegar together; rub into the chicken. Refrigerate for 15 minutes.

Heat the oil in a pan; stir-fry the gram flour till a pleasing smell emanates. Add chicken cubes and sauté on low heat for 3-5 minutes till half cooked.

Add breadcrumbs and mix well. Remove and spread on a clean table top to cool.

Skewer the cubes 2″ apart and roast in a tandoor till done. Bring the cubes close together and coat with egg yolk. Roast till the egg coating turns golden brown. Remove, garnish with onion rings and serve hot with mint chutney (see p.7).

Murg Jugalbandi

Stuffed chicken breasts in a thick curry

Ingredients

8 Chicken breasts

For the filling
200 gm / 7 oz Chicken, minced
2 tsp / 10 ml Vegetable oil
1 tsp / 3 gm Mustard seeds (*rai*)
a few Curry leaves (*kadhi patta*)
½ tsp / 2 gm Salt
1 tsp / 2 gm Red chilli powder
1 tsp / 2 gm *Garam masala*
2½ tbsp / 10 gm Coconut (*nariyal*),
    fresh, grated
Vegetable oil for frying

For the curry
4 tsp / 20 ml Vegetable oil
a pinch Cumin (*jeera*) seeds
1½ tsp / 9 gm Ginger (*adrak*) paste
1½ tsp / 9 gm Garlic (*lasan*) paste
Salt to taste
1 tsp / 2 gm Red chilli powder
1 tsp / 2 gm Turmeric (*haldi*) powder
4 tsp / 4½ gm Coriander (*dhaniya*)
    powder
¼ cup / 50 gm / 1¾ oz Yoghurt
    (*dahi*), whisked
¼ cup / 50 gm / 1¾ oz Tomato purée
50 gm / 1¾ oz Brown onion paste
    (see p. 7)
6 tbsp / 90 ml / 3 fl oz Water
1 Tomato, diced
1 tsp / 6 gm Black peppercorns
    (*sabut kali mirch*)

Method

Clean and wash the chicken breasts. Make deep incisions near the bone of the chicken breasts. Keep aside.

For the filling, heat the oil in a pan; add mustard seeds and curry leaves; sauté for a few seconds. Add the mince and cook for about 5-6 minutes.

Add salt, red chilli powder, *garam masala*, and coconut. Stir-fry for a few minutes. Remove from heat and keep aside to cool. Stuff the chicken breasts with the prepared mixture.

Heat the oil in a pan; add 2 stuffed chicken breasts, at a time, and sauté till golden brown on both sides. Remove and keep aside.

For the curry, heat the oil in a pan; add cumin seeds and sauté for a few seconds. Add ginger-garlic paste and sauté for 1 minute.

Add salt, red chilli powder, turmeric powder, and coriander powder; cook for another minute.

Stir in the yoghurt and tomato purée and stir-fry on medium heat. Add the brown onion paste and cook till the oil leaves the sides of the pan. Add water and bring to the boil; simmer and cook till the curry reduces to three-fourths of the original quantity.

Add the chicken pieces to the curry and allow to cook for 10-12 minutes. Remove from heat.

Carefully lift the chicken pieces from the curry and place on a serving platter. Pour the curry on top and serve hot, garnished with tomato and black peppercorns.

Murg Jalfrezi

Chicken cooked with tomatoes and capsicum

Ingredients

800 gm / 28 oz Chicken, boneless,
    cut into pieces
Vegetable oil for frying
$^1/_3$ cup / 100 gm / 3½ oz Onion paste
½ cup / 100 gm / 3½ oz Tomato
    purée
Salt to taste
3 tbsp / 54 gm / 1¾ oz Ginger
    (*adrak*) paste
3 tbsp / 54 gm / 1¾ oz Garlic (*lasan*)
    paste
½ cup / 60 gm / 2 oz Onions, diced
60 gm / 2 oz Tomatoes, diced
60 gm / 2 oz Capsicum (*Shimla
    mirch*), diced
2 tsp / 4 gm *Garam masala*

Method

Heat 1 tbsp oil in a wok (*kadhai*); add onion paste and cook for 5-7 minutes. Add tomato purée and cook for 10-15 minutes. Remove from heat and set aside.

Marinate the chicken pieces with salt and ginger and garlic pastes for 2 hours.

In a separate wok, heat the oil and add the onion mixture, tomatoes, and capsicum. Sauté for a few minutes, add the marinated chicken and stir-fry till the chicken is cooked. Sprinkle *garam masala*.

Serve hot, accompanied by a green salad.

Bharwan Tangri

Serves: 4
Preparation Time: 1 hr
Cooking Time: 15 min

Tandoori drumsticks stuffed with cottage cheese

Ingredients:

8 Chicken drumsticks
1 tsp / 2 gm White pepper (*safed mirch*) powder
Salt to taste
1 tsp / 6 gm Ginger (*adrak*) paste
1 tsp / 6 gm Garlic (*lasan*) paste

For the filling
150 gm / 5 oz Cottage cheese (*paneer*), mashed
4 Green chillies, finely chopped
1 tbsp / 4 gm Green coriander (*hara dhaniya*), finely chopped
1 tsp / 1½ gm Cumin (*jeera*) powder
½ tsp / 1 gm Yellow chilli powder
1 tbsp / 10 gm Cashew nuts (*kaju*), finely chopped
Salt to taste

For the coating
2 tbsp / 40 ml / 1¼ fl oz Cream
1 tbsp / 15 gm Cheese, grated
1 tbsp / 10 gm Cornflour
Butter for basting

Method

Clean the drumsticks. Make an incision along the lower half of the drumsticks, taking care not to cut through the other side. Carefully open the flap for the filling.

Mix white pepper, salt, ginger and garlic pastes; rub evenly over the drumsticks. Marinate for 30 minutes.

For the filling, mix cottage cheese, green chillies, green coriander, cumin powder, yellow chilli powder, cashew nuts, and salt together.

Put some filling into the flap of the marinated drumstick. Secure with a toothpick. Similarly, prepare the other drumsticks and refrigerate for 15 minutes.

For the coating, whisk the cream, cheese, and cornflour into a smooth paste. Coat each drumstick evenly with this paste.

Preheat oven / tandoor / grill to 180°C / 350°F. Skewer the drumsticks and roast for 8-10 minutes, basting occasionally with butter.

Remove and hang the skewers for 3-4 minutes to let the excess marinade drip off.

Roast again for 3-4 minutes till golden. Serve hot with mint chutney (see p. 7) and salad.

Murg Kandhari

Serves: 4
Preparation Time: 20 min
Cooking Time: 25 min

Chicken cooked in pomegranate juice

Ingredients:

700 gm / 24 oz Chicken, cut into boneless pieces
1 tbsp / 18 gm Ginger-garlic (*adrak-lasan*) paste
1½ tsp / 6 gm Salt
2 tsp / 4 gm Red chilli powder
3 tbsp / 45 ml / 1½ fl oz Vegetable oil
4 tbsp / 60 gm / 2 oz Cashew nut (*kaju*) paste
¼ cup / 50 gm / 1¾ oz Yoghurt (*dahi*)
1 cup / 250 ml / 8 fl oz Water
4 tsp / 20 gm Brown onion paste (see p. 7)
3 tbsp / 45 gm / 1½ oz Tomato purée
½ cup / 100 gm / 3½ oz Pomegranate seeds (*anar dana*)
½ cup / 50 ml / 1¾ fl oz Cream
½ tsp / 1 gm *Garam masala*

Method

Wash, clean and dry the chicken pieces. Marinate the chicken pieces with 2 tsp ginger-garlic paste, half of salt, and red chilli powder. Keep aside for 10-15 minutes.

Heat 2 tbsp oil in a pan; sauté the chicken pieces for a few minutes without letting the colour change. Keep aside.

Add the remaining oil to the pan, sauté the remaining ginger-garlic paste for 2-3 minutes. Add cashew nut paste mixed with yoghurt and water. Season with remaining salt and red chilli powder, simmer for 8-10 minutes.

Add the brown onion paste, tomato purée, and chicken pieces and cook on low heat till the chicken is tender and the curry has thickened.

Extract juice from pomegranate seeds and strain through a muslin cloth into the simmering curry.

Stir in the cream. Remove from heat, transfer to a serving dish, and serve hot, garnished with *garam masala*.

Murg-e-Khas

Chicken drumsticks stuffed with nuts

Ingredients

4 Chicken drumsticks, washed
300 gm / 11 oz Chicken, minced
5 tsp / 30 gm / 1 oz Ginger (*adrak*)
  paste
5 tsp / 30 gm / 1 oz Garlic (*lasan*)
  paste
Salt to taste
5 tsp / 25 gm Green chilli paste
2 tbsp / 30 ml / 1 fl oz Lemon
  (*nimbu*) juice
½ cup / 60 gm / 2 oz Almonds
  (*badam*)
½ cup / 60 gm / 2 oz Cashew nuts
  (*kaju*)
½ cup / 100 gm / 3½ oz Mint
  chutney (see p. 7)
1 tsp / 2 gm *Garam masala*
3 tsp / 15 ml Vegetable oil
1 tsp / 1 gm Saffron (*kesar*)
½ cup / 100 ml / 3½ fl oz Cream

Method

Debone the entire chicken leg, leaving only the top of the drumstick. Flatten the chicken leg using a steak hammer.

Make a marinade with half the quantity of ginger and garlic pastes, salt, green chilli paste, and lemon juice. Rub the paste into the chicken and refrigerate for 30 minutes.

Mix the almonds, cashew nuts, chicken mince, and mint chutney together.

Add *garam masala* and the remaining ginger, garlic, green chilli pastes, salt, and lemon juice to the mince mixture; mix well.

Stuff the deboned chicken with this mixture, rolling the chicken in such a way that the mince is wrapped in it.

Place the rolls on a greased tray and cover with foil. Bake in a medium-sized hot oven (100°C / 200°F) until done (approximately 20 minutes).

Take the chicken out of the oven and remove the foil. Slice each chicken roll diagonally and arrange on a platter.

Pour the saffron mixed with cream over the sliced chicken.

Serve hot, garnished with lemon wedges and tomato slices.

Khatta Murg

Tangy chicken

Ingredients

1 kg / 2.2 lb Chicken, deboned

For the marinade
1¼ cups / 250 gm / 9 oz Yoghurt (*dahi*)
2 tbsp / 36 gm / 1¼ oz Ginger (*adrak*) paste
2 tbsp / 36 gm / 1¼ oz Garlic (*lasan*) paste
1 tsp / 2 gm Cumin (*jeera*) seeds
1 tsp / 2 gm Black pepper (*kali mirch*) powder
2 tbsp / 30 ml / 1 fl oz Lemon (*nimbu*) juice
3 Green chillies, chopped
3 tbsp / 45 gm / 1½ oz Almond (*badam*) paste
150 gm / 5 oz Onions, cut into rings
100 gm / 3¼ oz Capsicum (*Shimla mirch*), cut into rings
2½ tbsp / 50 gm / 1¾ oz White butter
a pinch Saffron (*kesar*), dissolved in 1 tbsp milk
Salt to taste

Method

For the marinade, mix all the ingredients and rub into the chicken. Keep aside for 2 hours.

Place the chicken without overlapping in a greased, ovenproof shallow dish. Arrange onion and capsicum rings over the chicken and pour the leftover marinade, evenly.

Dot with white butter and roast in a preheated oven (150°C / 300°F) for about 20 minutes.

Remove the dish from the oven, sprinkle saffron, cover the dish and return back to the oven. Simmer for about 10 minutes more.

Uncover the dish, wipe the edges and simmer again for about 10 minutes. Serve hot with mint chutney (see p. 7).

Murg Chakori

Serves: 4
Preparation Time: 45 min
Cooking Time: 20 min

Chicken breasts stuffed with minced lamb

Ingredients

8 Chicken breasts
250 gm / 9 oz Lamb, minced
1 tsp / 2 gm Black cumin (*shah jeera*) seeds
1 tsp / 2 gm Ginger powder (*sonth*)
2 tsp / 4 gm Fennel (*moti saunf*) powder
1 tsp / 1½ gm Cumin (*jeera*) powder
1 tsp / 2 gm Red chilli powder
1 tsp / 1½ gm Coriander (*dhaniya*) powder
2 tsp / 8 gm Salt
¼ cup / 50 gm / 1¾ oz Yoghurt (*dahi*)
a pinch Asafoetida (*hing*)
1 cup / 200 ml / 7 fl oz Vegetable oil
1 cup / 250 ml / 8 fl oz Water

For the marinade

2½ cups / 500 gm / 1.1 lb Yoghurt (*dahi*), drained
Salt to taste
½ cup / 100 ml / 3½ fl oz Cream
1 tsp / 2 gm Red chilli powder
1½ tsp / 8 ml Vinegar (*sirka*)
1 tsp / 1½ gm Coriander powder

Method

Clean the chicken breasts, slit open from one side and flatten. Keep aside.

Blend together the lamb mince, black cumin seeds, dry ginger powder, fennel powder, cumin powder, red chilli powder, coriander powder, salt, yoghurt, and asafoetida.

Divide the mince mixture equally into 8 balls. In a pan, heat the oil and water in equal quantities, reduce heat and immerse the balls into the pan. Cover and cook for about 20 minutes.

Stuff the prepared meat balls into the chicken breasts. Wrap the chicken breasts firmly with silver foil. Poach (to cook in simmering liquid) for 15 minutes.

Remove from heat and unwrap the chicken breast from the foil and allow to cool.

For the marinade, blend yoghurt, salt, cream, red chilli powder, vinegar, and coriander powder together. Keep aside.

Marinate the chicken breasts with the prepared marinade and keep aside for 15 minutes.

Skewer the chicken breasts and cook in a tandoor for 5-10 minutes or until golden yellow.

Remove from the skewers and serve hot, accompanied by tandoori roti (see p. 127).

Kesar Murg

Saffron chicken

Ingredients

800 gm / 28 oz Chicken, boneless, cut into 8 pieces
½ cup / 100 ml / 3½ fl oz Vegetable oil
2 Bay leaves (*tej patta*)
6 Green cardamoms-cloves (*choti elaichi-laung*)
½ cup / 150 gm / 5 oz Onion paste
2 tbsp / 36 gm / 1¼ oz Ginger (*adrak*) paste
2 tbsp / 36 gm / 1¼ oz Garlic (*lasan*) paste
1 tsp / 1½ gm Coriander (*dhaniya*) powder
5 tbsp / 75 gm / 2½ oz Cashew nut (*kaju*) paste
1 cup / 200 gm / 7 oz Yoghurt (*dahi*), whisked
Salt to taste
1 tsp / 2 gm White pepper (*safed mirch*) powder
a pinch Saffron (*kesar*)
¾ cup / 150 ml / 5 fl oz Cream

Method

Heat the oil in a heavy-bottomed pan; add bay leaves, cloves, and green cardamoms; sauté until the cardamoms change colour.

Add onion, ginger, and garlic pastes; stir-fry till the oil separates.

Add coriander powder and cashew nut paste; stir-fry for 2 minutes.

Add the chicken and cook for 3 minutes. Mix in the yoghurt, salt, white pepper, and saffron. Bring to the boil, reduce heat and simmer until the chicken becomes tender.

Fold in the cream. Serve hot, accompanied by any Indian bread.

Adrak Kebab

Ginger chicken kebabs

Ingredients

1 kg / 2.2 lb Chicken breasts, cut
  into boneless cubes
1 tbsp / 15 gm Green chilli paste
2 tsp / 4 gm White pepper (*safed
  mirch*) powder
Salt to taste
3¼ tbsp / 60 gm / 2 oz Ginger (*adrak*)
  paste
4 tsp / 20 ml Malt vinegar (*sirka*)
1 cup / 200 gm / 7 oz Yoghurt (*dahi*),
  drained
4 tbsp / 80 ml / 2¾ fl oz Cream
Butter for basting
2 tsp / 12 gm Ginger, julienned

Method

Clean the chicken cubes. Mix green chilli paste, white pepper powder, salt, ginger paste, and vinegar in a large bowl and rub on the chicken cubes. Keep aside for 30 minutes.

Mix yoghurt and cream in a separate bowl. Add the chicken cubes and keep aside for 30 minutes.

Skewer chicken cubes and roast in a preheated (180°C / 350°F) oven / tandoor / grill for 5-8 minutes. Hang the skewers to allow the excess marinade to drip off. Roast again for 4-5 minutes. Remove from skewers.

Serve hot, garnished with ginger.

Murg Paneer Tikka

Chicken tikka marinated in cottage cheese

Ingredients

1 kg / 2.2 lb Chicken breasts, cut into boneless cubes
1 tbsp / 15 ml Lemon (*nimbu*) juice
3 tbsp / 54 gm / 1¾ oz Garlic (*lasan*) paste
Salt to taste
150 gm / 5 oz Cottage cheese (*paneer*), grated
4 tbsp / 80 ml / 2¾ fl oz Cream
1½ tbsp / 15 gm Cornflour
2 tsp / 10 gm Green chilli paste
1 tsp / 2 gm White pepper (*safed mirch*) powder
1 tbsp / 4 gm Green coriander (*hara dhaniya*), chopped
Butter for basting

Method

Marinate the chicken in lemon juice, garlic paste, and salt mixture for 1 hour.

Mix cottage cheese, cream, cornflour, green chilli paste, white pepper powder, and green coriander in a bowl; whisk till smooth. Marinate the chicken in this mixture for at least 3 hours.

Skewer chicken 2 cm apart and roast in a preheated (180°C / 350°F) oven / tandoor / grill for 8-10 minutes. Baste with butter and roast for another 3 minutes or until golden in colour.

Garnish with tomato, onion, and cucumber slices and serve hot with mint chutney (see p.7).

Murg Malai Tikka

Serves: 4
Preparation Time: 3½ hrs
Cooking Time: 15 min

Creamy chicken tikka

Ingredients

1 kg / 2.2 lb Chicken breasts, cut into boneless cubes
2 tbsp / 36 gm / 1¼ oz Garlic (*lasan*) paste
2 tbsp / 36 gm / 1¼ oz Ginger (*adrak*) paste
Salt to taste
1 tsp / 2 gm White pepper (*safed mirch*) powder
1 Egg, whisked
½ cup / 60 gm / 2 oz Cheddar cheese, grated
8 Green chillies, deseeded, finely chopped
1 cup / 25 gm Green coriander (*hara dhaniya*), finely chopped
½ tsp / 1 gm Mace-nutmeg (*javitri-jaiphal*) powder
1 tbsp / 10 gm Cornflour
¾ cup / 150 ml / 5 fl oz Cream
Vegetable oil / Butter for basting

Method

Rub garlic-ginger pastes, salt, and white pepper into the chicken cubes. Keep aside for 15 minutes.

Mix the remaining ingredients together (except oil / butter); coat the chicken with this prepared mixture. Marinate for at least 3 hours.

Skewer the chicken cubes 2 cm apart and roast in a preheated (140°C / 275°F) oven / grill / tandoor for 5-8 minutes. Remove and hang the skewers for 3-5 minutes to allow the excess marinade to drip off; brush with oil and roast again for 3 minutes.

Garnish with green coriander, tomato slices, and lemon wedges and serve hot with mint chutney (see p. 7).

Murg Kaju Kebab

Serves: 4
Preparation Time: 1 hr
Cooking Time: 15-20 min

Chicken drumsticks coated with cashew batter

Ingredients

12 Chicken drumsticks
4 tsp / 24 gm Ginger-garlic (*adrak-lasan*) paste
a pinch White pepper (*safed mirch*) powder
1 tsp / 4 gm Salt
1 tsp / 5 ml Vinegar (*sirka*)
1¼ cups / 250 gm / 9 oz Yoghurt (*dahi*)
¾ cup / 150 ml / 5 fl oz Cream
2 tbsp / 36 gm / 1¼ oz Ginger-garlic paste
1 tsp / 2 gm White pepper powder
2 tsp / 4 gm *Garam masala*
½ tsp / 2 gm Salt
a few strands Saffron (*kesar*)
Vegetable oil for basting
4 Eggs, whisked
5 tbsp / 75 gm / 2½ oz Cashew nuts (*kaju*), finely ground

Method

Wash and clean the chicken drumsticks. Make 4-5 deep vertical incisions.

Mix ginger-garlic paste, white pepper powder, salt, and vinegar together. Coat the drumsticks with this paste and rub into the slits. Refrigerate for 15 minutes.

Make a second marinade with yoghurt, cream, ginger-garlic paste, white pepper powder, *garam masala*, salt, and saffron.

Marinate the chicken in the prepared marinade and refrigerate for another 15 minutes.

Skewer the drumsticks and roast in a tandoor for 3-5 minutes or till half cooked. Remove and hang for 2-3 minutes to allow the excess marinade to drip off.

Baste with oil / butter and roast till completely cooked.

Mix the cashew nut paste and eggs together. Coat the drumsticks with this batter and roast again till the egg has coagulated. Remove from skewers.

Serve hot with mint chutney (see p. 7).

Murg Seekh Kebab

Chicken drumsticks stuffed with cottage cheese

Ingredients

1 kg / 2.2 lb Chicken, minced
2 Eggs
1 tbsp / 4½ gm Cumin (*jeera*)
  powder
1 tsp / 2 gm Yellow chilli powder
1 tsp / 2 gm White pepper (*safed
  mirch*) powder
Salt to taste
4 tsp / 20 ml Vegetable oil
4 tbsp / 60 gm / 2 oz Cashew nuts
  (*kaju*), pounded
2 tbsp / 48 gm / 1¾ oz Ginger
  (*adrak*), finely chopped
4 tsp / 24 gm Onions, chopped
5 tbsp / 20 gm Green coriander (*hara
  dhaniya*), finely chopped
1 tsp / 2 gm *Garam masala*
Vegetable oil for basting
Butter (unsalted) for brushing

Method

Whisk the eggs, add cumin powder, yellow chilli powder, white pepper powder, salt, and oil. Add to the mince and mix well. Keep aside for 10 minutes.

Add cashew nuts, ginger, onions, green coriander, and *garam masala*. Mix well. Divide into 10 equal portions.

With wet hands, wrap two portions along each skewer. Keep 2″ between each portion. Prepare 5 skewers like this.

Roast in a moderately hot tandoor or charcoal grill for about 6 minutes until golden brown in colour, or roast in a preheated oven at 150°C / 300°F for 8 minutes, basting with oil just once.

Remove from skewers and brush with butter.

Serve hot, garnished with onion rings and lemon wedges.

Murg Hara Pyaz

Serves: 4
Preparation Time: 20 min
Cooking Time: 45 min

Spring onion chicken

Ingredients

800 gm / 28 oz Chicken, cut into
  boneless cubes
5 tbsp / 75 ml / 2½ fl oz Mustard
  (*sarson*) oil
1 cup / 120 gm / 4 oz Onions,
  chopped
100 gm / 3½ oz Tomatoes, finely
  chopped
2 tsp / 6 gm Mustard seeds (*rai*)
Salt to taste
2 tsp / 3 gm Cumin (*jeera*) powder
Red chilli powder to taste
100 gm / 3½ oz Spring onions
  (*hara pyaz*)

Method

Heat 2 tbsp oil in a wok (*kadhai*); sauté the onions till transparent.
Add tomatoes and cook for 10-15 minutes. Keep aside.

In a separate wok, heat the remaining oil. Add the mustard seeds
and sauté till they crackle.

Stir in the onion-tomato mixture; cook for 3-4 minutes. Add the
chicken, salt, cumin powder, and red chilli powder.

Cook for another 20 minutes on low heat, till the chicken is done.

Mix in the spring onions and cook for 2 minutes.

Remove from heat and serve hot.

Neza Kebab

Chicken legs flavoured with green cardamom

Ingredients

900 gm / 2 lb Chicken drumsticks

For the marinade
5 tbsp / 90 gm / 3 oz Ginger (*adrak*)
  paste
5 tbsp / 90 gm / 3 oz Garlic (*lasan*)
  paste
1½ tsp / 6 gm Salt
2 tsp / 4 gm White pepper (*safed
  mirch*) powder
2 tsp / 4 gm *Garam masala*
1 tsp / ½ gm Dry fenugreek (*kasoori
  methi*) powder
4 tsp / 20 ml Vinegar (*sirka*)
2 cups / 50 gm / 1¾ oz Green
  coriander (*hara dhaniya*), chopped
2 tsp / 4 gm Green cardamom (*choti
  elaichi*) powder

4 tbsp / 60 ml / 2 fl oz Vegetable oil
3 cups / 300 gm / 11 oz Gram flour
  (*besan*)
4 Eggs, whisked
1 cup / 200 ml / 7 fl oz Cream
Butter for basting

Method

Wash and clean the chicken drumsticks. Detach the thigh bone from the flesh.

For the marinade, mix all the ingredients together and rub into the chicken. Marinate for 20 minutes.

Heat the oil in a pan; add gram flour and stir-fry on low heat till a pleasing smell emanates. Remove from heat and transfer to a mixing bowl to cool.

Add 1 egg and blend to make a smooth paste; add cream and mix well.

Add the remaining eggs to the mixture and mix thoroughly. Coat the chicken drumsticks with this marinade and keep aside for 20 minutes.

Skewer the drumsticks once along the bone and once through the thigh flesh. Cook in a tandoor for about 8-10 minutes or till slightly coloured. Remove and let the excess marinade drip off.

Baste lightly with butter and roast again for 2-3 minutes or till completely done.

Remove from skewers onto a serving platter. Serve hot garnished with lemon wedges, cucumber and tomato dices, and onion rings.

Murg Kali Mirch

Chicken with black pepper

Ingredients

800 gm / 28 oz Chicken drumsticks
2 tsp / 12 gm Ginger (*adrak*) paste
2 tsp / 6 gm Garlic (*lasan*) paste
½ tsp / 1 gm Turmeric (*haldi*) powder
2 tsp / 10 gm Red chilli paste
Salt to taste
Vegetable oil for frying
2 tsp / 12 gm Black peppercorns (*sabut kali mirch*), crushed
3 tbsp / 45 ml / 1½ fl oz Lemon (*nimbu*) juice
4 tsp Green coriander (*hara dhaniya*), chopped
½ tsp / 1 gm *Garam masala*

Method

Mix together ginger-garlic paste, turmeric powder, red chilli paste, and salt.

Marinate the chicken drumsticks in this mixture and keep aside for 2 hours.

Heat the oil in a pan; fry the chicken till golden brown in colour. Remove and keep aside.

In a wok (*kadhai*), add chicken along with the marinade and all the remaining ingredients. Stir-fry till the chicken is fully cooked. Serve hot, accompanied by any Indian bread.

Tandoori Murg

Tandoori chicken

Ingredients

1 (750 gm / 26 oz) Chicken, cut into
4 pieces, washed, pat dried

For the first marinade
1½ tbsp / 22 ml Lemon (*nimbu*) juice
1 tsp / 2 gm Red chill powder
Salt to taste

For the second marinade
½ cup / 100 gm / 3¼ oz Yoghurt
(*dahi*)
1 tbsp / 18 gm Garlic (*lasan*) paste
1 tbsp / 18 gm Ginger (*adrak*) paste
½ tsp / 1 gm Black salt (*kala namak*)
1 tsp / 2 gm *Garam masala*
a few drops Red colour
Salt to taste

½ tsp Dry fenugreek leaves (*kasoori
methi*), powdered
2 Onions, cut into rings
1 Lemon, cut into wedges

Method

Make 2 deep incisions each on the breasts, thighs, and drumsticks.

For the first marinade, mix all the ingredients mentioned and rub on the chicken pieces and also inside the incisions. Keep aside for 1 hour.

For the second marinade, mix all the ingredients mentioned in a bowl and rub the chicken pieces; keep aside for 3-4 hours to marinate.

Preheat the oven to 180°C / 350°F. Place the chicken on the grill rack or wire rack (place a tray underneath to collect the drippings) and grill for 8-10 minutes. Brush the pieces with oil, turn them around and grill for 8-10 minutes more till the chicken is dry and cooked. Remove from oven, sprinkle dry fenugreek powder and serve with onion rings and lemon wedges.

Murg Badam Pasanda

Serves: 4
Preparation Time: 1 hr
Cooking Time: 40 min

Chicken breasts garnished with fried almonds

Ingredients

8 pieces Chicken breasts, skinned
½ cup / 100 gm / 3¼ oz Ghee
5 tsp / 25 gm Almonds (*badam*),
   sliced
3 tbsp / 54 gm / 1¾ oz Ginger
   (*adrak*) paste
1½ cups / 300 gm / 11 oz Yoghurt
   (*dahi*), hung
3 tbsp / 54 gm / 1¾ oz Garlic (*lasan*)
   paste
Salt to taste
10 Green cardamoms (*choti elaichi*)
10 Cloves (*laung*)
¾ cup / 90 gm / 3 oz Onions,
   chopped
300 gm / 11 oz Tomatoes
1 tsp / 2 gm Red chilli powder
2 tsp Refined flour (*maida*)
1 tsp / 2 gm Black pepper (*kali mirch*)
   powder
4 cups / 1 lt / 32 fl oz Chicken stock
   (see p. 7)
1 tsp / 2 gm Mace (*javitri*) powder
a pinch Saffron (*kesar*), dissolved in
   1 tbsp milk
5 tbsp / 20 gm Green coriander (*hara*
   dhaniya)

Method

Brown the almonds in 1 tbsp ghee.

Clean and flatten the chicken breasts till about 3 cm thick.

Rub the ginger paste over the chicken breasts.

Whisk the yoghurt in a large bowl, add garlic paste and salt. Rub this mixture over the chicken and keep aside for 1 hour.

Heat half the ghee on a griddle. Place the chicken breasts on it and cook, turning over once, until half done. Remove and keep aside.

Heat the remaining ghee in a pan and sauté green cardamoms and cloves till they crackle. Then add onions and cook till brown. Add tomatoes, red chilli powder, flour, black pepper, and chicken stock. Cook until the gravy becomes rich and thick.

Place the chicken breasts in the gravy and cook, turning it over gently, for another 10 minutes.

Add the mace powder and saffron mixture.

Serve, garnished with fried almonds and green coriander.

Tandoori Chicken Chaat

Shredded chicken in a lemon dressing

Ingredients

2 Tandoori chicken (see p.45), shredded
1 tbsp / 15 ml Lemon (*nimbu*) juice
Salt to taste
1 tsp / 2 gm Red chilli powder
1 tbsp / 15 ml Vegetable oil
½ cup / 100 gm / 3½ oz Raw green mangoes, cut into strips
½ cup / 60 gm / 2 oz Onions, finely sliced
2 tsp / 10 gm Green chillies, chopped
2 cups / 50 gm / 1¾ oz Green coriander (*hara dhaniya*), chopped
2 tsp / 4 gm *Chaat masala*
1 tsp Ginger (*adrak*), chopped

Method

Prepare a lemon dressing by mixing together lemon juice, salt, red chilli powder, and oil. Keep aside.

In a mixing bowl, add raw mangoes, onions, green chillies, green coriander, *chaat masala*, shredded chicken, and the lemon dressing. Mix well.

Remove to a serving bowl and serve immediately, garnished with ginger.

Fish & Seafood

Saloni Macchi Tikka

Serves: 4
Preparation Time: 40 min
Cooking Time: 15-20 min

Smoked fish chunks in a spicy marinade

Ingredients

800 gm / 28 oz Fish, cut into
  boneless pieces

For the marinade
1 tbsp / 6 gm Salt
1 tsp / 2 gm White pepper (*safed
  mirch*) powder
½ tsp Fenugreek (*methi*) powder
½ tsp / 1 gm Turmeric (*haldi*)
  powder
1½ tsp / 3 gm Red chilli powder
1 tsp / 2 gm *Garam masala*
a pinch Clove (*laung*) powder
5 tsp / 30 gm / 1 oz Ginger-garlic
  (*adrak-lasan*) paste
2 tsp / 10 gm Yoghurt (*dahi*), drained
¾ cup / 150 ml / 5 oz Vinegar (*sirka*)
½ cup / 100 ml / 3½ fl oz Cream

4 tbsp / 60 ml / 2 fl oz Mustard
  (*sarson*) oil
16 Cloves
1 Charcoal piece, live
Vegetable oil for basting

Method

Wash, clean and dry the fish pieces.

For the marinade, mix all the ingredients together and rub on the
fish pieces and keep aside.

Make a well in the centre and put mustard oil and cloves. Place the
live charcoal piece in the oil and cover the bowl with a lid. Seal the
lid so that the smoke does not escape. Keep aside for 30 minutes.

Remove the lid, skewer the fish and roast in a medium-hot tandoor
for 5-6 minutes. Remove from the tandoor and allow the excess
marinade to drip off.

Baste with oil and roast again for 2 minutes until done. Remove
from skewers and transfer to a serving platter.

Serve hot accompanied by a green salad and mint chutney
(see p. 7).

52 ~ Fish & Seafood

Jhinga Mehrunisa

Serves: 4
Preparation Time: 40 min
Cooking Time: 10 min

Tandoori prawns in a rich creamy marinade

Ingredients

1 kg / 2.2 lb Prawns, shelled, deveined
3 tbsp / 45 ml / 1½ fl oz Vinegar (*sirka*)
Salt to taste

For the marinade
4 tsp / 20 ml Lemon (*nimbu*) juice
1¼ cups / 250 gm / 9 oz Yoghurt (*dahi*)
1 cup / 200 ml / 7 fl oz Cream
1½ tsp / 3 gm White pepper (*safed mirch*)
  powder
¾ cup / 90 gm / 3 oz Cheese, grated
2 tsp / 1 gm Dry fenugreek (*kasoori
  methi*) powder
2 tbsp / 36 gm / 1¼ oz Ginger-garlic
  (*adrak-lasan*) paste
1½ tsp / 3 gm *Garam masala*
a few strands Saffron (*kesar*)
Butter for basting

Method

Wash the prawns with vinegar and salt water. Drain and pat dry.

For the marinade, mix all the ingredients together (except butter). Rub on the prawns and marinate for 30 minutes.

Skewer the prawns and roast in a moderately hot tandoor for 6-8 minutes. Remove from tandoor and allow the excess marinade to drip off.

Baste lightly with butter and roast again for 2-3 minutes. Remove from skewers and serve with mint chutney (see p. 7).

Fish & Seafood ~ 55

Jhinga Til Tikka

Crispy sesame prawns

Ingredients

1 kg / 2.2 lb King prawns, shelled,
  deveined
Vegetable oil for frying

For the first marinade
4 tsp / 24 gm Ginger (*adrak*) paste
5 tsp / 30 gm / 1 oz Garlic (*lasan*)
  paste
1 tsp / 2 gm Red chilli powder
1 tsp / 5 ml Lemon (*nimbu*) juice

For the second marinade
4 tbsp / 60 gm / 2 fl oz Cheddar
  cheese, grated
1 tbsp Carom (*ajwain*) seeds
4 tbsp / 60 ml / 2 fl oz Cream
½ tsp / 1 gm Green cardamom (*choti
  elaichi*) powder
½ tsp / 1 gm Mace (*javitri*) powder
3 tbsp / 30 gm / 1 oz Gram flour
  (*besan*), roasted
½ cup / 100 gm / 3½ oz Yoghurt
  (*dahi*), drained
¼ cup Sesame (*til*) seeds
½ cup / 60 gm / 2 oz Breadcrumbs,
  dried, powdered

Method

Mix all the ingredients of the first marinade and rub into the prawns. Keep aside for 30 minutes. Squeeze the prawns gently to remove the excess moisture.

Whisk together the ingredients of the second marinade (except sesame seeds and breadcrumbs) and marinate the prawns in this mixture for another 30 minutes.

Make a mixture of breadcrumbs and sesame seeds. Coat the prawns with the mixture and refrigerate for 15-20 minutes.

Heat the oil in a wok (*kadhai*) till it starts smoking. Lower heat and fry the prawns for 1-2 minutes. Remove, drain and keep aside for 4-5 minutes. Deep-fry again till they are crisp and golden in colour. Remove and drain the excess oil and serve hot, garnished with lemon wedges.

Saunfiya Jhinga

Serves: 4
Preparation Time: 20 min
Cooking Time: 20 min

Fennel-flavoured prawns

Ingredients

12 Prawns, deveined, shelled
1 tbsp / 20 gm Butter
2 tsp / 4 gm Fennel (*moti saunf*),
  broiled, pounded
2 tsp / 6 gm Garlic (*lasan*), chopped
5 Green chillies, deseeded, chopped
2 tbsp / 50 gm / 1¾ oz Onion paste
2 tbsp / 30 ml / 1 fl oz Lemon
  (*nimbu*) juice
Salt to taste
½ cup / 100 ml / 3½ fl oz Cream
½ cup / 100 gm / 3½ oz Yoghurt
  (*dahi*)
1 tsp / 6 gm Ginger (*adrak*), chopped

Method

Heat the butter in a pan and sauté the fennel seeds for a few seconds.

Add garlic, green chillies, and onion paste. Stir-fry for a few minutes.

Mix in all the other ingredients and cook for 5-10 minutes. Remove from heat.

Place the prawns in an ovenproof dish; pour the prepared mixture on top. Cover the dish tightly and cook in a preheated (180°C / 350°F) oven for 15-20 minutes.

Remove from the oven. Transfer onto a serving platter and serve immediately accompanied by steamed rice.

Jalpari Kebab

Saffron-flavoured fish rolls stuffed with prawns

Ingredients

12 Fish fillets, thin
220 gm / 8 oz Prawns, shelled,
  deveined
5 tsp / 30 gm / 1 oz Ginger-garlic
  (*adrak-lasan*) paste
5 tsp / 25 gm Mango pickle masala
1 tsp / 1½ gm Carom (*ajwain*) seeds
1 tsp / 2 gm White pepper (*safed
  mirch*) powder
2 tsp / 4 gm *Garam masala*
Salt to taste
1 tsp / 2 gm Red chilli powder
1 tsp / 5 ml Lemon (*nimbu*) juice
4 tsp / 20 ml Vegetable oil
¾ cup / 150 gm / 5 oz Yoghurt (*dahi*),
  drained
2 tbsp / 40 ml / 1¼ oz Cream
a few strands Saffron (*kesar*)
a pinch Green cardamom (*choti
  elaichi*) powder
4 cups / 1 lt / 32 fl oz Water

Method

Extract juice from ginger-garlic paste and keep aside.

Clean the fish fillets and prawns. Pat dry with a cloth.

Make a marinade with ginger-garlic paste, mango pickle masala, half of carom seeds, white pepper powder, *garam masala*, salt, red chilli powder, lemon juice, and oil.

Marinate the fish fillets in the prepared marinade and keep aside for 5 minutes.

Prepare second marinade of yoghurt, cream, saffron, green cardamom powder, and remaining half of other ingredients. Keep aside.

Put one fish fillet flat on a tabletop. Place a prawn at one end of the fillet and roll the fillet. Wrap it tightly with cling wrap or aluminium foil.

Boil water in a pot and cook the rolls for 10 minutes keeping the pot covered.

Drain the water and place the rolls under running water for 1 minute. Remove the foil.

Marinate the rolls in the second marinade for 5 minutes.

Skewer the rolls and roast in hot tandoor or in an oven (150°-180°C / 300°-350°F) for 10 minutes.

Remove from skewers, transfer to a serving platter and serve hot with mint chutney (see p.7).

Doi Maach

Bengali style fish with yoghurt

Ingredients

1 kg / 2.2 lb Fish, Rohu fillets,
   washed
1½ cups / 300 gm / 11 oz Yoghurt
   (*dahi*)
½ tsp / 1 gm Turmeric (*haldi*)
   powder
¼ cup / 50 gm / 1¾ oz Ghee
2 Cloves (*laung*)
2 Green cardamoms (*choti elaichi*)
1 Cinnamon (*dalchini*), 1″ stick
1 Bay leaf (*tej patta*)
5 Black peppercorns (*sabut kali
   mirch*)
½ cup / 60 gm / 2 oz Onions,
   chopped
3 tbsp / 54 gm / 1¾ gm Ginger
   (*adrak*) paste
1 tsp / 2 gm Red chilli powder
Salt to taste
¾ cup / 90 gm / 3 oz Raisins
   (*kishmish*)

Method

Marinate the fillets in half the yoghurt and turmeric powder for half an hour.

Heat the ghee and sauté the fish till it is three-fourth done. Keep aside.

To the ghee, add cloves, green cardamoms, and cinnamon stick, bay leaf, and black peppercorns. Sauté for a few seconds, then add onions and ginger paste. Cook till the onions brown a little.

Add the remaining yoghurt, red chilli powder, and enough water to cover the ingredients.

Return the fish to the pan and then simmer for at least 15 minutes or until done.

Season with salt, add raisins and serve.

Macchi Rolls

Serves: 4
Preparation Time: 30 min
Cooking Time: 40 min

Fish rolls

Ingredients

12 Fish (2″ x 4″ strips)
4 tbsp / 80 gm / 2¾ oz Butter
4 Onions, chopped
3 Green chillies, slit
2 tsp / 12 gm Ginger (*adrak*),
  chopped
½ tsp / 1 gm Turmeric (*haldi*)
  powder
1 cup / 200 gm / 7 oz Yoghurt (*dahi*),
  whisked
½ cup / 100 ml / 3½ fl oz Cream
½ tsp / 1½ gm Fenugreek seeds
  (*methi dana*), broiled, powdered
½ tsp / 1 gm Green cardamom (*choti
  elaichi*) powder
1 tsp Green coriander (*hara dhaniya*),
  chopped

Method

Roll each fish strip and secure with a toothpick.

Heat the butter in a heavy-bottomed pan; sauté onions until soft.
Add green chillies and ginger; stir-fry for a few minutes.

Add turmeric powder, yoghurt, cream, fenugreek seeds, and green
cardamom powder; sauté for 10-15 minutes.

Place the fish rolls in the sauce and cook on low heat (*dum*) for 10-
15 minutes or until the fish is cooked. Remove from heat. Transfer
the fish into a serving dish and remove the toothpicks.

Strain the gravy and pour on top of the fish. Serve hot, garnished
with green coriander.

Nariyal Chingri

Shrimps flavoured with coconut   Picture on facing page

Ingredients

600 gm / 22 oz Shrimps, peeled
6 tbsp / 90 ml / 3 fl oz Vegetable oil
1 tsp / 3 gm Mustard seeds (*rai*)
2 Curry leaves (*kadhi patta*)
2 tsp / 6 gm Garlic (*lasan*), slivered
4 Onions, chopped
1 Green chilli, chopped
1 tsp / 1½ gm Coriander (*dhaniya*) powder
1 tsp / 2 gm Red chilli powder
1 tsp / 2 gm Turmeric (*haldi*) powder
1 Coconut (*nariyal*), fresh, grated
2 tsp / 4 gm Cumin (*jeera*) seeds
Salt to taste
1 cup / 200 ml / 7 fl oz Coconut milk

Method

Heat the oil in a wok (*kadhai*); sauté mustard seeds till they crackle. Add curry leaves, garlic, and onions. Stir-fry till the onions turn transparent.

Stir in all the other ingredients except coconut milk. Cook till the oil separates and appears on the surface. Add water as and when necessary to cook the curry.

Add the coconut milk along with the shrimps. Stir-fry till the shrimps are cooked and the curry has thickened. Remove from heat.

Serve hot.

Aam Chingri

Shrimps with mangoes

Ingredients

400 gm / 14 oz Shrimps
1 tsp / 2 gm Turmeric (*haldi*) powder
Salt to taste
½ cup / 100 ml / 3½ fl oz Vegetable oil
1 tsp / 3 gm Mustard seeds (*rai*)
4 Curry leaves (*kadhi patta*)
100 gm / 3½ oz Onions, chopped
2 Green chillies, slit
1 tbsp / 24 gm Ginger (*adrak*), chopped
1 tbsp / 12 gm Garlic (*lasan*), chopped
1 tbsp / 4½ gm Coriander (*dhaniya*)
   powder
2 tsp / 4 gm Red chilli powder
200 gm / 7 oz Mangoes, raw, sliced
1 cup / 200 ml / 7 fl oz Coconut
   (*nariyal*) milk (see p.7)

Method

Marinate the shrimps in turmeric powder and salt; keep aside.

Heat the oil in a wok (*kadhai*); sauté shrimps for a while. Remove and keep aside.

Add mustard seeds in the same oil and let them crackle.

Add curry leaves, onions, green chillies, ginger, and garlic. Cook till the onions are lightly browned. Add coriander powder and red chilli powder; stir.

Mix the shrimps and mangoes into the curry. Add the coconut milk and cook for 15-20 minutes or till the curry thickens.

Remove from heat.

Tawa Macchi

Serves: 4
Preparation Time: 20 min
Cooking Time: 30 min

Stir-fried fish cooked on a griddle

Ingredients

1 kg / 2.2 lb Fish, cut into boneless
  pieces
½ cup / 100 gm / 3½ oz Ghee
1 tsp / 1½ gm Carom (*ajwain*) seeds
100 gm / 3½ oz Onions, chopped
2 tsp / 12 gm Ginger (*adrak*),
  chopped
4 Green chillies, chopped
1 tsp / 2 gm Red chilli powder
1 tsp / 1½ gm Coriander (*dhaniya*)
  powder

For the gravy

¼ cup / 50 gm / 1¾ oz Ghee
4 tsp / 24 gm Garlic (*lasan*) paste
2 tsp / 3 gm Coriander powder
1 tsp / 2 gm Red chilli powder
4 Green chillies, chopped
2 tbsp / 48 gm / 1¾ oz Ginger,
  julienned
100 gm / 3½ oz Tomatoes, julienned
1 tsp Dry fenugreek (*kasoori methi*)
  powder
Salt to taste
500 gm / 1.1 lb Tomatoes, chopped
1 tsp / 2 gm *Garam masala*
2 tbsp / 8 gm Green coriander (*hara
  dhaniya*), chopped

Method

For the gravy, heat the ghee in a wok (*kadhai*); add garlic paste and sauté for a few minutes.

Add all the other ingredients for the gravy except *garam masala* and green coriander and cook till the gravy thickens. Remove from heat and keep aside.

Heat the ghee on a griddle (*tawa*); add the fish pieces and sauté till half done. Remove the fish pieces to the sides of the griddle.

Add carom seeds and sauté. Add onions along with all the ingredients and the fried fish. Stir-fry for a few minutes. Stir in the gravy and cook till the gravy dries.

Sprinkle *garam masala* and green coriander. Remove from heat and serve hot.

Meen Molee

Tangy fish cooked in coconut milk

Ingredients

750 gm / 26 oz Fish, cleaned, spiced
1 tsp / 2 gm Turmeric (*haldi*) powder
1½ tsp / 4½ gm Garlic (*lasan*),
   chopped
1 Dry red chilli (*sookhi lal mirch*)
2 Coconuts (*nariyal*), grated
4 tbsp / 60 ml / 2 fl oz Vegetable oil
2 Onions, medium-sized
1 Ginger (*adrak*), 1″ piece
6 Green chillies, slit
1 tbsp / 15 ml Lemon (*nimbu*) juice
Salt to taste
250 gm / 9 oz Tomatoes, big,
   chopped

Method

Grind the turmeric powder, ½ tsp garlic, and the skin of dry red chilli together.

Make 2 extractions of coconut milk: the first extraction 1½ cups and the second 2 cups (see p. 7).

Heat the oil in a pot; add the onions, ginger, green chillies, and the remaining garlic; sauté for a few minutes. Add the ground paste and sauté.

Pour the second extract of coconut milk, lemon juice, and salt. When it comes to the boil, add the fish and cook on low heat for half an hour.

When the fish is cooked, add the first extract of coconut milk and arrange the tomatoes on top. Bring to the boil and remove the pot from the heat. Serve hot.

Chingri Maacher Curry

Serves: 4
Preparation Time: 45 min
Cooking Time: 30 min

Prawns cooked in coconut milk

Picture on facing page

Ingredients

900 gm / 2 lb Prawns, shelled
3 tsp / 6 gm Turmeric (*haldi*) powder
3 tsp / 12 gm Salt
½ cup / 100 ml / 3½ fl oz Creamed coconut
2 cups / 500 ml / 16 fl oz Water
½ cup / 100 ml / 3½ fl oz Vegetable oil
1 Onion, large, chopped
1 tsp / 2 gm Red chilli powder
1 tsp / 3 gm Sugar
3 Green chillies, chopped

Method

Marinate the prawns in salt and turmeric powder. Keep aside for half an hour.

Blend together the creamed coconut and water. Keep aside.

Heat the oil in a wok (*kadhai*); fry the prawns on high heat until golden brown. Remove with a slotted spoon and keep aside. To the same oil, add onion and fry till golden brown. Add red chilli powder and cook for 2-3 minutes.

Add the coconut-milk mixture and bring to the boil. Add the prawns and green chillies. Cover and cook on low heat for 20 minutes or until the gravy thickens. Serve hot.

Kalonji Macchi

Serves: 4
Preparation Time: 20 min
Cooking Time: 15-20 min

Fish flavoured with onion seeds in coconut sauce

Ingredients

4 Fish fillets (sole / plain), cut into 3 pieces each
2 tbsp / 30 ml / 1 fl oz Vegetable oil
1 tsp / 1½ gm Onion seeds (*kalonji*)
4 Dry red chillies (*sookhi lal mirch*)
3 Garlic (*lasan*) cloves, sliced
1 Onion, medium-sized, sliced
2 Tomatoes, medium-sized, sliced
¼ cup / 25 gm Coconut (*nariyal*), grated
Salt to taste
1 tsp / 1½ gm Coriander (*dhaniya*) powder
½ cup / 175 ml / 6 fl oz Water
1 tbsp / 15 ml Lemon (*nimbu*) juice
1 tbsp / 4 gm Green coriander (*hara dhaniya*), chopped

Method

Heat the oil in a wok (*kadhai*); reduce heat and add onion seeds, dry red chillies, garlic, and onion. Stir-fry for 3-4 minutes.

Mix in the tomatoes, coconut, salt, and coriander powder.

Add the fish pieces to the mixture and turn gently to cook evenly. Simmer and cook for 5-7 minutes.

Stir in the water, lemon juice, and green coriander. Cook further for 3-5 minutes or until the water evaporates.

Remove to a serving dish and serve hot.

Tandoori Pomfret

Serves: 4
Preparation Time: 3 hrs
Cooking Time: 15 min

Marinated pomfret cooked in a tandoor   Picture on facing page

Ingredients

4 (450 gm / 1 lb each) Pomfrets
2 tbsp / 60 gm / 2 oz Yoghurt (*dahi*), drained
2 Egg yolks
3 tbsp / 60 ml / 2 fl oz Cream
1 tbsp / 18 gm Ginger (*adrak*) paste
1 tbsp / 18 gm Garlic (*lasan*) paste
2 tsp / 3 gm Carom (*ajwain*) seeds
1 tsp / 2 gm White pepper (*safed mirch*) powder
2 tsp / 4 gm Red chilli powder
1 tsp / 2 gm Turmeric (*haldi*) powder
2 tsp / 3 gm Cumin (*jeera*) powder
2 tbsp / 20 gm Gram flour (*besan*)
2 tbsp / 30 ml / 1 fl oz Lemon (*nimbu*) juice
Butter / Vegetable oil for basting

Method

Clean and wash the fish. Make 2-3 incisions on both sides.

Whisk together the yoghurt and egg yolks with the remaining ingredients to make a smooth paste.

Coat the fish evenly with the yoghurt paste and leave to marinate for at least 3 hours.

Preheat oven to 180°C / 350°F. Skewer the fish from mouth to tail. Roast for 10 minutes. Remove from heat and hang the skewers to drain the excess liquid. Baste with butter and roast again for 3-5 minutes.

Serve at once, accompanied by a salad.

Lahsuni Tikka

Serves: 4
Preparation Time: 1½ hrs
Cooking Time: 20 min

Garlic-flavoured fish tikka

Ingredients

1 kg / 2.2 lb Fish fillets, cut into cubes
Salt to taste
1 tbsp / 15 ml Lemon (*nimbu*) juice
½ cup / 100 gm / 3½ oz Yoghurt (*dahi*)
1 tbsp / 15 ml Vinegar (*sirka*)
1 tbsp Garam masala
2 tsp / 4 gm Cumin (*jeera*) seeds, ground
1 tsp / 1½ gm Carom (*ajwain*) seeds
1 tsp / 2 gm Red chilli powder
2 tsp / 12 gm Garlic (*lasan*) paste
Vegetable oil / Butter for basting

Method

Wash and dry the cubed fish fillets. Sprinkle salt and lemon juice. Keep aside to marinate for half an hour.

In a bowl, combine yoghurt with the remaining ingredients (except oil) and whisk well. Pour the mixture over the fish cubes and coat evenly. Leave to marinate for at least one hour.

Preheat oven to 180°C / 350°F. Roast, bake or grill till the fillets are golden brown in colour and cooked through, basting just once.

Serve hot.

Lamb

Shola Kebab

Spicy aromatic lamb chunks

Ingredients

900 gm / 2 lb Lamb, cut into
  boneless pieces
4 tsp / 16 gm Salt
4 tsp / 8 gm Red chilli powder
a pinch White pepper (*safed mirch*)
  powder
a pinch Fenugreek (*methi*) powder
a pinch Green cardamom (*choti
  elaichi*) powder
2 tsp / 4 gm *Garam masala*
2 tsp / 3 gm Onion seeds (*kalonji*),
  crushed
a pinch Fennel (*moti saunf*), crushed
a pinch Mustard seeds (*rai*), crushed
a pinch Cumin (*jeera*) seeds, crushed
a pinch Coriander (*dhaniya*) seeds,
  crushed
2 tbsp / 36 gm / 1¼ oz Ginger-garlic
  (*adrak-lasan*) paste
60 gm / 2 oz Raw papaya, grated
½ cup / 100 ml / 3½ fl oz Mustard
  (*sarson*) oil
4 tsp / 20 ml Vinegar (*sirka*)
½ cup / 100 gm / 3½ oz Yoghurt
  (*dahi*)
4 tsp / 20 gm Butter for basting

Method

Prepare the marinade by mixing all the ingredients (except butter) together.

Rub the mixture into the lamb pieces and keep aside for 1½ hours.

Skewer the lamb pieces and roast in a medium-hot tandoor for 10-12 minutes. Baste with butter and roast again for 5 minutes.

Remove from skewers and serve hot.

Peshawari Kebab

Serves: 4
Preparation Time: 1½ hrs
Cooking Time: 30 min

Succulent lamb cubes

Ingredients

1 kg / 2.2 lb Lamb, boneless, cut into
    1˝ cubes

For the marinade
½ cup / 100 gm / 3½ oz Yoghurt
    (*dahi*)
2 tsp / 10 gm Raw papaya paste
Salt to taste
2 tsp / 4 gm Red chilli powder
1 tsp / 2 gm *Garam masala*
1 tsp / 2 gm Black cumin (*shah jeera*)
    seeds
1 tbsp / 18 gm Ginger (*adrak*) paste
1 tsp / 6 gm Garlic (*lasan*) paste

Ghee for basting
1 tsp / 2 gm *Chaat masala*
1 Juice of lemon (*nimbu*)

Method

For the marinade, mix all the ingredients and rub well into the lamb. Leave aside for an hour.

Skewer the meat pieces and cook in a tandoor till half done.

Remove and leave to cool for 10 minutes.

Baste with ghee and cook for 8 more minutes.

Sprinkle with *chaat masala* and lemon juice.

Serve hot with a green salad.

Masala Tandoori Gosht

Serves: 4
Preparation Time: 2½ hrs
Cooking Time: 20 min

Spicy lamb steaks

Ingredients

8 Lamb steaks (2˝ x 2˝)

For the marinade
1 Onion, minced
1 tbsp / 18 gm Garlic (*lasan*),
    crushed
1 tbsp / 15 gm Green chilli paste
1 tbsp Poppy seeds (*khus khus*),
    ground
1 tbsp / 5 gm *Garam masala*
Salt to taste

Method

For the marinade, mix all the ingredients together. Rub into the lamb steaks. Marinate for 2 hours.

Roast in charcoal grill / tandoor till cooked as desired.

Serve hot, garnished with onion rings and accompanied by pickled green chillies.

Sakhat Kebab

Lamb kebabs stuffed with cheese

Ingredients

900 gm / 2 lb Lamb, minced
1 tsp / 4 gm Salt
a pinch White pepper (*safed mirch*)
  powder
½ tsp / 1 gm Red chilli powder
a pinch Fenugreek (*methi*) powder
2 tbsp / 36 gm / 1¼ oz Ginger-garlic
  (*adrak-lasan*) paste
1½ tsp Green chillies, chopped
1 tbsp / 4 gm Green coriander (*hara
  dhaniya*), chopped

For the filling
¾ cup / 150 gm / 5 oz Processed
  cheese, grated
4 tsp Green chillies, chopped

For the batter
6 tbsp / 60 gm / 2 oz Cornflour
6 tbsp / 60 gm / 2 oz Refined flour
  (*maida*)
1 Egg, whisked
1 tsp / 5 ml Vinegar (*sirka*)
Salt to taste
a pinch White pepper powder
1½ tsp / 9 gm Ginger-garlic paste
1 cup / 250 ml / 8 fl oz Water
Vegetable oil for frying

Method

Mix the lamb mince with salt, white pepper powder, red chilli powder, fenugreek powder, ginger-garlic paste, green chillies, and green coriander. Refrigerate for 15 minutes.

For the filling, mix the 2 ingredients together and divide into 16 equal portions.

For the batter, mix cornflour with flour, egg, vinegar, salt, white pepper powder, ginger-garlic paste, and water.

Make 10 cm-long kebabs with the mince mixture and skewer in 4 equal parts. Roast in a tandoor for 5 minutes and remove. Allow to cool, remove from skewers.

Slit each kebab lengthwise and stuff the cheese mixture.

Dip the stuffed kebabs in the prepared batter and deep-fry in hot oil until crisp and golden brown. Remove and drain the excess oil on paper towels.

Serve hot with mint chutney (see p.7).

Shammi Kebab

Serves: 4
Preparation Time: 1 hr
Cooking Time: 30 min

Melt-in-the-mouth lamb patties

Ingredients

1 kg / 2.2 lb Lamb, finely minced,
   without any fat
1¼ cups / 200 gm / 7 oz Bengal gram
   (*chana dal*), soaked for ½ hour
1 tsp / 2 gm Cumin (*jeera*) seeds
1 Ginger (*adrak*), 1″ piece
1 Onion, medium-sized sliced,
   browned
1 tbsp / 6 gm Coriander (*dhaniya*)
   seeds, powdered
2 tsp / 4 gm *Garam masala*
2 Eggs
4 Green chillies, chopped
1 tbsp / 4 gm Green coriander (*hara
   dhaniya*), chopped
Salt to taste
Vegetable oil for frying
1 Onion, cut into rings
10 Mint (*pudina*) leaves

Method

Add the lamb mince, drained Bengal gram, cumin seeds, ginger, and ½ cup water in a pressure cooker; cook till you hear the first whistle.

Turn off the flame, but do not open the cooker till the pressure dies down completely.

Now open the cooker, return to heat and cook till the mixture is completely dry. Remove and keep aside to cool.

When the mixture is cool enough to handle, add the browned onion and coriander powder. Grind the mixture on a stone slab or in a mixer.

Add the eggs, green chillies, green coriander, and salt. Mix well.

Divide the paste into 20 portions. Make small, round patties; slightly flatten them between your palms.

Refrigerate for 30 minutes before frying, to avoid the patties from breaking while frying.

Heat the oil in a wok (*kadhai*); deep-fry the patties, a few at a time, till brown. Remove with a slotted spoon and drain the excess oil on absorbent kitchen paper towels.

Serve hot garnished with onion rings and mint leaves.

Note: *When the minced meat has fat in it, the kebabs or koftas will not bind properly. Always add the eggs a little at a time, to avoid getting a sticky paste. Very often one needs less egg than prescribed in the recipe.*

Lamb Chops

Potato-coated lamb chops

Ingredients

12 Lamb chops
2 cups / 500 ml / 16 fl oz Water
1 Onion, medium-sized, sliced
1 tsp / 6 gm Ginger (*adrak*), sliced
6 Garlic (*lasan*) cloves
6-8 Black peppercorns (*sabut kali mirch*)
1 Cinnamon (*dalchini*), 1″ stick
2 Black cardamoms (*badi elaichi*)
4 Cloves (*laung*)
Salt to taste

For the coating
500 gm / 1.1 lb Potatoes, boiled, peeled, mashed
1 tsp / 6 gm Ginger, finely chopped
2 Green chillies, finely chopped
1 tbsp / 4 gm Green coriander (*hara dhaniya*), chopped
½ tsp / 1 gm Black pepper (*kali mirch*) powder
½ tsp / 1 gm Red chilli powder
Salt to taste
Breadcrumbs, powdered

Method

Put the chops in a pan. Add water, onion, ginger, garlic, black peppercorns, cinnamon stick, black cardamoms, cloves, and salt. Cover the pan and let the chops simmer on low heat till tender. Remove from the stock and keep aside.

For the coating, add ginger, green chillies, green coriander, black pepper powder, red chilli powder, and salt to the potatoes. Mix well.

Divide the potato mixture into 12 portions.

With wet palms, spread one portion of the potato mixture. Place a chop in the middle and wrap the mashed potato around it, shaping it well. Prepare the remaining chops similarly and keep aside.

Spread the powdered breadcrumbs on a flat tray. Coat each chop evenly with the breadcrumbs and keep aside.

Heat the oil in a wok (*kadhai*) till it starts smoking; fry the chops, two at a time, till crisp and nicely browned from all sides. Remove and drain the excess oil on paper towels and serve with salad.

Khatta Pudina Chops

Tangy mint lamb chops

Ingredients

1 kg / 2.2 lb Lamb chops, cleaned
1 tsp / 1½ gm Cumin (*jeera*) powder
1 tbsp / 5 gm White pepper (*safed mirch*)
2 tsp / 4 gm *Garam masala*
5 tsp / 25 ml Lemon (*nimbu*) juice
Salt to taste
4 tbsp / 80 ml / 2¾ fl oz Cream
¾ cup / 150 gm / 5 oz Yoghurt (*dahi*), drained
1¼ cups / 250 gm / 9 oz Mint chutney (see p.7)
2 tbsp / 20 gm Cornflour
3 tbsp / 45 gm / 1½ oz Papaya paste (optional)
1 tbsp / 18 gm Garlic (*lasan*) paste
1 tbsp / 18 gm Ginger (*adrak*) paste
1 tsp / 2 gm Fenugreek (*methi*) powder
Vegetable oil for basting

Method

Mix cumin powder, white pepper, *garam masala*, lemon juice, and salt together. Rub the paste into the lamb chops and marinate for 1 hour.

Mix cream, yoghurt, mint chutney, and cornflour. Add the remaining ingredients (except oil) and whisk to a fine paste. Mix with lamb chops and marinate for another 2½-3 hours.

Skewer lamb chops, 2 cm apart, and roast in a preheated (180°C / 350°F) oven / tandoor / charcoal grill for 8-10 minutes. Hang the skewers for a few minutes to allow the excess marinade to drip off. Baste with oil and roast for another 4-5 minutes.

Sprinkle lemon juice, garnish with slices of cucumber, tomato, and onion; serve hot.

Raan

Serves: 4
Preparation Time: 2½ hrs
Cooking Time: 1½ hrs

Roast leg of lamb flavoured with yoghurt

Ingredients

1 Leg of lamb

For the marinade
4 tbsp / 100 gm / 3½ oz Brown onion paste
2 tsp / 12 gm Garlic (*lasan*) paste
2 tsp / 12 gm Ginger (*adrak*) paste
½ tsp / 1 gm Green cardamom (*choti elaichi*) powder
4 tbsp / 120 gm / 4 oz Yoghurt (*dahi*)
2 tsp / 4 gm Red chilli powder
Salt to taste
½ tsp / 1 gm *Garam masala*
1 tsp / 2 gm Black pepper (*kali mirch*) powder
a pinch Saffron (*kesar*)

Vegetable oil for basting
Chaat masala to taste

Method

Clean the leg of lamb and prick thoroughly down to the bone with a fork. Mix all the ingredients of the marinade together. Apply evenly on the lamb and leave to marinate for 2 hours.

Place the leg in a baking tray with 2 cups water. Bake in a preheated (180°C / 350°F) oven for at least 1 hour turning the leg twice / thrice to ensure that the leg cooks evenly. Roast till the liquid dries up.

Baste with oil and grill / roast in a moderately-hot tandoor till well done.

Sprinkle *chaat masala* and garnish with onion rings. Serve with mint chutney (see p.7).

Khada Masala Gosht

Serves: 4
Preparation Time: 20 min
Cooking Time: 2 hrs

Lamb cooked with whole spice

Ingredients

1 kg / 2.2 lb Lamb, cut into pieces
½ cup / 100 ml / 3½ fl oz Vegetable oil
2 Onions, finely chopped
1 tsp / 2 gm Fennel (*moti saunf*) seeds
1 tsp / 1½ gm Coriander (*dhaniya*) powder
1 tsp / 1½ gm Cumin (*jeera*) powder
8 Cloves (*laung*)
1 Cinnamon (*dalchini*), 2″ stick
5 Green cardamoms (*choti elaichi*)
1 tbsp / 18 gm Ginger (*adrak*) paste
1 tbsp / 18 gm Garlic (*lasan*) paste
Salt to taste
1½ cups / 250 gm / 9 oz Yoghurt (*dahi*)
½ tsp / 1 gm *Garam masala*

Method

Heat the oil in a pan; add the onions, sauté till light brown. Add the whole and powdered spices, lamb, ginger paste, garlic paste, salt, and yoghurt; mix well.

Cover with a thick lid that can hold about 1 cm of water on it, and cook on low heat for 2 hours.

Remove the lid and continue to cook if you want a dry preparation.

Add *garam masala*, mix well and serve hot.

Note: *This is* dum pukht *style of cooking. The lamb cooks in its own juices and as long as there is water on the lid, the ingredients inside the pan will never burn.*

Kallan Kebab

Skewered rolls of lamb liver and kidney with chicken mince

Ingredients

250 gm / 9 oz Lamb, minced
120 gm / 4 oz Lamb kidney, finely
  chopped
120 gm / 4 oz Lamb liver, finely
  chopped
½ tsp / 2 gm Salt
2 tsp / 4 gm Red chilli powder
1 tsp / 2 gm *Garam masala*
a pinch Fenugreek (*methi*) powder
2 tsp / 12 gm Ginger-garlic (*adrak-
  lasan*) paste
1 tbsp / 4 gm Green coriander (*hara
  dhaniya*), chopped
1 tsp Green chillies, chopped
500 gm / 1.1 lb Chicken, minced
½ tsp / 2 gm Salt
½ tsp / 1 gm White pepper (*safed
  mirch*) powder
a pinch *Garam masala*
a pinch Fenugreek powder
½ tsp / 3 gm Ginger-garlic paste
1 tbsp / 4 gm Green coriander,
  chopped
4 tsp / 20 gm Butter for basting

Method

Mix the lamb mince, kidney, liver, salt, red chilli powder, *garam masala*, fenugreek powder, ginger-garlic paste, green coriander, and green chillies together. Keep aside.

Skewer the lamb mince mixture and roast in a charcoal grill for 8-10 minutes. Remove from the grill, place the skewer upright to allow the excess moisture to drip off. Keep aside for 3-5 minutes.

Meanwhile, mix chicken mince with the remaining ingredients (except butter).

Apply a coating of the chicken mince mixture evenly over the lamb mince kebabs and roast again for 5-6 minutes.

Baste with butter and remove the kebabs from the skewers in 4 equal portions.

Serve immediately, accompanied by a green salad and mint chutney (see p. 7).

Handi Pasanda

Serves: 4
Preparation Time: 30 min
Cooking Time: 30 min

Lamb steaks cooked in a slow oven

Ingredients

750 gm / 26 oz Lamb escallops
  (2″ x 4″)
½ cup / 100 ml / 3½ fl oz Vegetable oil
1 cup / 120 gm / 4 oz Onions, sliced
3 tbsp / 36 gm / 1¼ oz Garlic (*lasan*)
  cloves, chopped
1 tbsp / 24 gm Ginger (*adrak*), chopped
1 tbsp Poppy (*khus khus*) seeds
2 Black cardamoms (*badi elaichi*)
1 Cinnamon (*dalchini*), 1″ stick
1 Bay leaf (*tej patta*)
6 Cloves (*laung*)
1 cup / 200 gm / 7 oz Yoghurt (*dahi*)
1 tsp / 2 gm Red chilli powder
1 tsp / 2 gm *Garam masala*
½ tsp / 1 gm Green cardamom (*choti
  elaichi*) powder
½ tsp / 1 gm Black pepper (*kali mirch*)
  powder

Method

Heat the oil in a pan; sauté half the onions till golden brown. Remove.

Mix garlic and ginger with browned and raw onions and poppy seeds. Blend to a fine paste with 2 tbsp water.

Reheat the oil and crackle the whole spices. Add onion paste mixture and sauté for 3-4 minutes. Add yoghurt and cook for 4-5 minutes. Add lamb and cook for another 3-4 minutes or till the oil separates. Transfer to a casserole. Add ½ cup water and sprinkle the spices. Cover and cook in a preheated oven at 140°C / 275°F for 10 minutes.

Serve hot garnished with green coriander.

Masaledaar Gosht

Slow cooked spicy lamb

Ingredients

1 kg / 2.2 lb Lamb, cut into pieces
¾ cup / 150 gm / 5 oz Yoghurt (*dahi*)
¾ cup / 150 ml / 5 fl oz Vegetable oil
Salt to taste
2 Bay leaves (*tej patta*)
3 Black cardamoms (*badi elaichi*)
8 Green cardamoms (*choti elaichi*)
1 cup / 120 gm / 4 oz Onions,
    chopped
3 tbsp / 54 gm / 1¾ oz Ginger
    (*adrak*) paste
3 tbsp / 54 gm / 1¾ oz Garlic (*lasan*)
    paste
5 tsp / 7½ gm Coriander (*dhaniya*)
    powder
½ tsp / 1 gm Turmeric (*haldi*)
    powder
1 tsp / 2 gm Red chilli powder
150 gm / 5 oz Tomatoes, chopped
4 tsp Garlic, chopped
4 tsp Ginger, shredded
2 tsp / 3 gm Cumin (*jeera*) powder
4 Dry red chillies (*sookhi lal mirch*)

Method

Whisk yoghurt and salt together and marinate the lamb in it for an hour.

Heat the oil in a pot (*handi*); add bay leaves and both the cardamoms; sauté till they crackle.

Add the onions and sauté till light brown. Add ginger and garlic pastes and stir for 4-5 minutes. Stir in coriander powder, turmeric powder, and red chilli powder.

Add the lamb along with the excess marinade and bring to the boil. Reduce heat and simmer adding 3 tsp water at regular intervals. Cook until the lamb is tender.

Add the tomatoes, garlic, and ginger; stir. Then add the cumin powder and dry red chillies. Cook on low heat till the lamb pieces are tender and evenly coated with the marinade.

Remove form heat and serve hot, accompanied by any Indian bread.

Baoli Handi

Boneless lamb with mushrooms and vegetables

Ingredients

900 gm / 2 lb Lamb, cut into
  boneless cubes
¾ cup / 150 ml / 5 fl oz Vegetable oil
2 Cinnamon (*dalchini*), 1˝ sticks
5 Cloves-Green cardamoms (*laung-
  choti elaichi*)
1 Nutmeg (*jaiphal*), powdered
2 tbsp / 36 gm / 1¼ oz Ginger-garlic
  (*adrak-lasan*) paste
1 cup / 120 gm / 4 oz Onions,
  chopped
1½ tsp / 6 gm Salt
1 tsp / 2 gm Red chilli powder
1 tsp / 1½ gm Coriander (*dhaniya*)
  powder
1 tsp / 2 gm Turmeric (*haldi*) powder
200 gm / 7 oz Carrots (*gajar*), cut
  into rounds
1 cup / 200 gm / 7 oz Tomato purée,
  fresh
30 gm / 1 oz Wholemilk fudge
  (*khoya*)
7 tsp / 45 gm / 1½ oz Brown onion
  paste (see p.7)
100 gm / 3½ oz Green peas (*hara
  matar*), shelled
80 gm / 2¾ oz Mushrooms (*guchhi*),
  stems removed
½ cup / 60 gm / 2 oz Cashew nuts
  (*kaju*), whole
2½ tbsp / 50 gm / 1¾ oz Yoghurt
  (*dahi*)
2 tsp / 4 gm *Garam masala*
4 cups / 1 lt / 32 fl oz Water

Method

Heat the oil in a pot; add cinnamon sticks, cloves, green cardamoms, and nutmeg; sauté till they crackle. Add ginger-garlic paste and sauté again for a few more minutes.

Add lamb and onions. Cook on medium heat till the liquid dries. Add salt, red chilli powder, coriander powder, turmeric powder, and carrots.

Stir in tomato purée and cook till the oil separates.

Mix in wholemilk fudge, brown onion paste, green peas, mushrooms, cashew nuts, yoghurt, and *garam masala*. Add water and cover the dish with a layer of dough. Reduce heat and cook till the meat is tender and the gravy has thickened.

Serve hot accompanied with steamed rice.

Gosht Pyaza

Lamb cooked with onions

Ingredients

1 kg / 2.2 lb Lamb, cut into pieces
4 tsp / 20 gm Butter
300 gm / 11 oz Button onions
½ cup / 100 ml / 3½ fl oz Vegetable oil
3 tsp / 6 gm Turmeric (*haldi*) powder
3 Bay leaves (*tej patta*)
10 Cloves (*laung*)
5 Cinnamon (*dalchini*), 1″ sticks
5 Dry red chillies (*sookhi lal mirch*)
10 Green cardamoms (*choti elaichi*)
200 gm / 7 oz Onions, chopped / sliced
3 tbsp / 54 gm / 1¾ oz Ginger (*adrak*) paste
2 tbsp / 36 gm /1¼ oz Garlic (*lasan*) paste
300 gm / 11 oz Tomatoes, blanched, deseeded, chopped
2½ tsp / 5 gm *Garam masala*
2 tsp / 3 gm Coriander (*dhaniya*) powder
4 tsp / 6 gm Cumin (*jeera*) powder
1½ tsp / 3 gm Mace (*javitri*) powder
a pinch Nutmeg (*jaiphal*) powder
2 tsp / 4 gm Black peppercorns (*sabut kali mirch*), crushed
Salt to taste
1 tbsp / 4 gm Green coriander (*hara dhaniya*), chopped
1 tsp Ginger, julienned

Method

Blanch the button onions and fry in hot butter for a few minutes.

Heat the oil in a pan; add turmeric powder, bay leaves, cloves, cinnamon sticks, dry red chillies, and green cardamoms; sauté on medium-heat for a few seconds until they begin to crackle.

Add the onions and sauté until soft and golden in colour. Stir in the ginger and garlic pastes and chopped tomatoes; cook for 5 minutes.

Add the lamb pieces and cook for 10-15 minutes on medium heat until a pleasant aroma comes from the lamb. Reduce heat, simmer on low heat and cook until the lamb is tender.

Sprinkle *garam masala*, coriander powder, cumin powder, mace powder, nutmeg powder, and black pepper powder. Season to taste. Add the button onions, stir, cover and cook for 2-3 minutes.

Serve hot, garnished with green coriander and julienned ginger.

Gosht ka Kofta

Lamb dumplings in tomato curry

Ingredients

For the dumplings
1 kg / 2.2 lb Lamb, minced
3 tbsp / 45 gm / 1¼ oz Butter
2 tsp / 3 gm Coriander (*dhaniya*) powder
150 gm / 5 oz Dried apricots, diced
2 tsp / 4 gm Fennel (*saunf*) powder
4 tsp / 24 gm Garlic (*lasan*) paste
4 tsp / 24 gm Ginger (*adrak*) paste
2 Green chillies, finely chopped
2 tbsp / 8 gm Green coriander, (*hara dhaniya*) finely chopped
120 gm / 4 oz Onions, grated
Salt for seasoning
2 tsp / 4 gm White pepper (*safed mirch*) powder

For the curry
½ cup / 100 ml / 3½ fl oz Vegetable oil
2 Bay leaves (*tej patta*)
10 Cloves (*laung*)
10 Green cardamoms (*choti elaichi*)
3 Cinnamon (*dalchini*), 1″ sticks
150 gm / 5 oz Onion paste
3 tbsp / 54 gm / 1¾ oz Garlic paste
3 tbsp / 54 gm / 1¾ oz Ginger paste
2 tsp / 10 gm Red chilli powder
350 gm / 12 oz Tomatoes, blanched, deseeded, chopped
Salt for seasoning
1 tbsp / 4 gm Green coriander (*hara dhaniya*), chopped
2 tsp / 4 gm *Garam masala*
2 tsp / 10 ml Cream
a pinch Saffron (*kesar*) strands, dissolved in 1 tbsp milk
2 tsp / 4 gm Mace (*javitri*) powder
3 drops Vetivier (*kewda*) essence

Method

Mix all the ingredients for the dumplings (except apricots) until the mixture sticks to the spoon. Season to taste with salt. Divide this mixture into 25 balls.

Stuff each meat ball with a diced apricot.

For the gravy, heat the oil in a pan; add bay leaves, cloves, green cardamoms and cinnamon sticks; sauté on medium heat for 30 seconds.

Stir in onion paste, ginger and garlic pastes; sauté for 30 seconds. Add red chilli powder, stir and cook for 3-4 minutes. Mix in tomatoes, stir and cook.

Add salt and green coriander; simmer on medium heat until the oil separates from the tomato curry.

Slip the dumplings into the curry along with 1½ cups hot water. Sprinkle *garam masala*, cover the pan and simmer for 10 minutes.

Add cream, the saffron mixture, mace powder and vetivier and remove from heat.

Serve hot.

Vegetarian

Paneer Seekh Kebab

Serves: 4
Preparation Time: 20 min
Cooking Time: 10 min

Skewered cottage cheese kebab

Ingredients

1 kg / 2.2 lb Cottage cheese (*paneer*),
   grated
30 gm / 1 oz Green chillies, chopped
2 Onions, grated
1 tbsp / 18 gm Ginger (*adrak*),
   coarsely ground
2 tbsp / 8 gm Green coriander (*hara
   dhaniya*), chopped
2 tsp / 4 gm Black pepper (*kali mirch*)
1 tsp / 1½ gm Cumin (*jeera*) powder
1 tsp / 2 gm Red chilli powder
Salt to taste
2 tbsp / 20 gm Cornflour
Butter for basting

Method

Mix all the ingredients, adding the cornflour in the end. Knead well.

With wet hands wrap the cottage cheese mixture around the skewers to form 4-5″-long kebabs. Each kebab should be 2 cm apart.

Roast in a preheated (150°C / 300°F) oven / tandoor / charcoal grill for 5-6 minutes, basting occasionally with melted butter.

Serve hot with salad and mint chutney (see p. 7).

Dum Aloo Kashmiri

Serves: 4
Preparation Time: 30 min
Cooking Time: 40 min

Kashmiri-style, slow-cooked potatoes

Ingredients

8 Potatoes, medium-sized
½ cup / 100 ml / 3½ fl oz Vegetable oil
1 tsp / 2 gm Black cumin (*shah jeera*) seeds
1 tsp / 2 gm Aniseed (*saunf*)
2 Onions, chopped
1 tsp / 2 gm Black cardamom (*badi elaichi*), pounded
5 tbsp / 50 gm / 1¾ oz Raisins (*kishmish*)
5 tbsp / 50 gm / 1¾ oz Cashew nuts (*kaju*)
Sate to taste

For the curry

2 tbsp / 50 gm / 1¾ oz Onion, chopped
1¼ cups / 250 gm / 9 oz Yoghurt (*dahi*), whisked
1 cup / 200 ml / 7 fl oz Tomato purée
4 tsp / 24 gm Ginger-garlic (*adrak-lasan*) paste
2¾ tbsp / 40 gm / 1¼ oz Almond (*badam*) paste
1 tsp / 2 gm Aniseed
½ tsp / 1 gm Mace (*javitri*) powder
½ tsp / 1 gm Black cumin seeds
4 Green cardamoms (*choti elaichi*)
6 Cloves (*laung*)
4 tsp / 20 gm Red chilli paste
2 tsp / 3 gm Cumin (*jeera*) powder
1 tbsp / 4½ gm Coriander (*dhaniya*) powder
Salt to taste
Vegetable oil for frying

Method

Peel the potatoes and slice off the tops. Scoop out the centre with a sharp knife. Fry the shells and centres to a golden brown. Allow the centres to cool and then mash.

Heat the oil in a wok (*kadhai*); sauté black cumin seeds and aniseed. Add onions and sauté till transparent. Add the fried potato centres, cardamom powder, raisins, and cashew nuts. Stir-fry for a few minutes. Season with salt. Keep aside.

Stuff the fried shells with the prepared mixture and keep aside.

For the curry, heat the oil in a thick-bottomed pan. Sauté onion till transparent. Add yoghurt, tomato purée, ginger-garlic paste, almond paste, aniseed, mace, black cumin seeds, green cardamoms, cloves, red chilli paste, cumin powder, coriander powder, and salt. Stir-fry for 8-10 minutes.

Place the stuffed potatoes in the curry; cover the lid and seal with dough. Cook on low heat for 10 minutes. Remove from heat. Place the potatoes in a serving dish, strain the curry and pour on top of the potatoes.

Serve immediately, accompanied by any Indian bread of choice.

Paneer Akbari

Stuffed cottage cheese fingers in thick gravy

Ingredients

600 gm / 22 oz Cottage cheese
(*paneer*), cut into 16 finger-sized
pieces

For the filling
4 tsp / 25 gm Wholemilk fudge
(*khoya*)
2 tbsp / 30 gm / 1 oz Cottage cheese,
mashed
2 tsp / 10 gm Cashew nuts (*kaju*),
chopped
1 tsp / 5 gm Pickle masala
4 tsp / 20 gm Tomato purée, thick

For the batter
3 tbsp / 30 gm / 1 oz Cornflour
Salt to taste
a few drops Yellow colour
Water as required

For the gravy
2 tsp / 10 ml + for frying Vegetable
oil
2 tsp / 12 gm Ginger-garlic (*adrak-lasan*) paste
2½ cups / 500 ml / 16 fl oz Tomato
purée, fresh
Salt to taste
½ tsp / 1 gm Red chilli powder
a pinch White pepper (*safed mirch*)
powder
a pinch Fenugreek (*methi*) powder
2 tsp / 4 gm *Garam masala*
2 tsp / 10 gm Butter
4 tsp / 20 ml Cream

Method

For the filling, mix together all the ingredients mentioned thoroughly. Stuff this filling between two cottage cheese fingers.

For the batter, mix together all the ingredients mentioned and make a smooth batter. Dip the cottage cheese sandwich in the batter and deep-fry in hot oil for 2-3 minutes. Remove with a slotted spoon and drain the excess oil on absorbent kitchen towels. Keep aside.

For the gravy, heat the oil in a pan; sauté the ginger-garlic paste for 2-3 minutes. Add the tomato purée and cook for 8-10 minutes until the mixture thickens. Add the seasoning and spices. Cook for 3-5 minutes. Stir in the butter and cream. Mix and remove from heat.

Arrange the fried cottage cheese sandwiches on a platter and pour the gravy on top.

Serve hot.

Shahi Paneer

Cottage cheese in an exotic curry

Ingredients

1 kg / 2.2 lb Cottage cheese (*paneer*), cut into fingers
5 tbsp / 75 ml / 2½ fl oz Vegetable oil
6 Cloves (*laung*)
2 Bay leaves (*tej patta*)
3 Cinnamon (*dalchini*), 1˝ sticks
6 Green cardamoms (*choti elaichi*)
1 cup / 300 gm / 11 oz Onion paste
2 tbsp / 36 gm / 1¼ oz Ginger (*adrak*) paste
2 tbsp / 36 gm / 1¼ oz Garlic (*lasan*) paste
2 tsp / 4 gm Red chilli powder
½ tsp / 1 gm Turmeric (*haldi*) powder
1 tsp / 1½ gm Coriander (*dhaniya*) powder
2 tbsp / 20 gm Cashew nut (*kaju*) paste
Salt to taste
a few drops Red food colouring
1¼ cups / 250 gms Yoghurt (*dahi*), whisked
½ cup / 125 ml / 4 fl oz Water, warm
2 tsp / 6 gm Sugar
½ cup / 100 ml / 3½ fl oz Cream
1 tsp / 2 gm *Garam masala*
½ tsp / 1 gm Green cardamom powder
1 tsp / 3 gm Mace (*javitri*) powder
3 drops Vetivier (*kewda*) essence
a few strands Saffron (*kesar*), dissolved in 1 tbsp milk
1 tbsp / 4 gm Green coriander (*hara dhaniya*), chopped

Method

Heat the oil in a pan; add cloves, bay leaves, cinnamon sticks, and green cardamoms. Sauté on medium heat. When they begin to crackle, add the onion paste and stir-fry for 2-3 minutes.

Stir in the ginger and garlic pastes, red chilli powder, turmeric powder, coriander powder, cashew nut paste, salt, and red colour.

Add the yoghurt, warm water, and sugar. Bring the mixture to a slow boil and then simmer until the oil separates.

Let the curry cool, remove the whole spices and blend to a smooth consistency.

Reheat the curry, stir in the cream, *garam masala*, cardamom powder, mace powder, vetivier, and saffron mixture.

Add cottage cheese and cook further for 5 minutes.

Serve hot garnished with green coriander.

Punjabi Kadhi

Creamy yoghurt curry with gram flour dumplings

Ingredients

For the dumplings (*pakora*)
²/₃ cup / 100 gm / 3½ oz Gram flour (*besan*)
½ cup / 60 gm / 2 oz Onions, chopped
1 tbsp / 25 gm Ginger (*adrak*), chopped
4-5 Green chillies, chopped
½ tsp / 2 gm Salt
¼ tsp / 1½ gm Baking powder
Vegetable oil for frying

For the *kadhi*
²/₃ cup / 100 gm / 3½ oz Gram flour
1 kg / 2.2 lb Yoghurt (*dahi*)
Salt to taste
1 tsp / 2 gm Turmeric (*haldi*) powder
½ cup / 100 ml / 3½ fl oz Mustard (*sarson*) oil
10 Dry red chillies (*sookhi lal mirch*)
1 tsp / 2 gm Coriander (*dhaniya*) seeds
1 tsp / 3 gm Fenugreek seeds (*methi dana*)
1 tsp / 3 gm Mustard seeds (*rai*)
1 tsp / 2 gm Cumin (*jeera*) seeds
¼ tsp / 1 gm Asafoetida (*hing*)
15-20 Curry leaves (*kadhi patta*)

For the tempering
2 tbsp / 30 gm / 1 oz Ghee
2 tsp / 4 gm Red chilli powder

Method

For the pakora, mix the gram flour with onions, ginger, green chillies, salt, and baking powder. Add just enough water to make a thick batter. Divide the batter into lemon-sized balls and keep aside.

Heat the oil in a wok (*kadhai*); carefully slide in the balls and deep-fry till golden brown. Remove with a slotted spoon and drain the excess oil on absorbent kitchen towels. Keep aside.

For the kadhi, mix the gram flour with yoghurt. Add salt and turmeric powder.

Heat the mustard oil till it starts smoking; add dry red chillies, coriander seeds, fenugreek seeds, mustard seeds, and cumin seeds. When they crackle, add asafoetida.

Now add the gram flour mixture and curry leaves. Cook on low heat for 2 hours.

For the tempering, heat the ghee and remove from heat. Add the red chilli powder and immediately pour this to the above mixture. Add the dumplings and serve hot

Baida Kebab

Skewered egg and potato rolls

Picture on facing page

Ingredients

200 gm / 7 oz Potatoes, boiled, mashed
10 Eggs, hard-boiled, grated
1 tsp / 2 gm *Garam masala*
1 tsp / 2 gm *Chaat masala*
½ cup / 60 gm / 2 oz Breadcrumbs
1½ tsp / 6 gm Salt
1 tsp / 2 gm Red chilli powder
2 tsp / 12 gm Ginger (*adrak*), chopped
1 tsp Green chillies, chopped
1 tbsp / 4 gm Green coriander (*hara dhaniya*),
  chopped
1 Egg
2 tbsp / 40 gm Butter for basting

Method

Mix together the eggs, potatoes, *garam masala*, *chaat masala*, breadcrumbs, salt, red chilli powder, ginger, green chillies, green coriander, and raw egg.

Divide this mixture into 5 equal portions

Wrap each portion along the length of the skewers with wet hands leaving a 2 cm gap between each. Roast for 5-10 minutes.

Remove and baste with butter. Roast further for 3-5 minutes or until cooked.

Remove from skewers and serve hot with mint chutney (see p. 7).

Vegetable Jalfrezi

Mixed vegetables

Ingredients

120 gm / 4 oz French beans
120 gm / 4 oz Cabbage (*bandh gobhi*)
120 gm / 4 oz Capsicum (*Shimla mirch*)
120 gm / 4 oz Carrots (*gajar*)
½ cup / 60 gm / 2 oz Onions
120 gm / 4 oz Potatoes, cut into fingers
4 tbsp / 60 ml / 2 fl oz Vegetable oil
1 tsp / 2 gm Cumin (*jeera*) seeds
2 Dry red chillies (*sookhi lal mirch*)
Salt to taste
½ tsp / 1 gm Black pepper (*kali mirch*) powder
2 tsp / 12 gm Ginger (*adrak*), chopped
4 tbsp / 60 ml / 2 fl oz Tomato purée
1 tbsp / 15 ml White vinegar (*sirka*)
1 tbsp / 4 gm Green coriander (*hara dhaniya*),
  chopped

Method

Chop beans, cabbage, capsicum, carrots and onions.

Heat the oil in a pan; add cumin seeds and dry red chillies. Sauté for a few seconds. Add all the vegetables, salt, black pepper powder, and ginger. Mix well. Cook covered on low heat till the vegetables are almost tender.

Add the tomato purée and white vinegar. Cook till the vegetables are completely done. Remove from heat.

Serve hot garnished with green coriander.

Palak Paneer Kofta

Cottage cheese koftas in spinach curry

Ingredients

For the koftas

500 gm / 1.1 lb Cottage cheese
   (*paneer*), mashed
250 gm / 9 oz Potatoes, boiled,
   mashed
3½ tbsp / 35 gm / 1¼ oz Cornflour
Salt to taste
½ tsp / 1 gm White pepper (*safed
   mirch*) powder
Vegetable oil for frying

For the gravy

1 kg / 2.2 lb Spinach (*palak*)
3½ tbsp / 35 ml / 1¼ oz Vegetable oil
1 tsp / 3 gm Garlic (*lasan*), chopped
½ cup / 100 ml / 3½ fl oz Tomato
   purée
½ tsp / 1 gm Red chilli powder
½ tsp / 1 gm Turmeric (*haldi*)
   powder
½ tsp / ¾ gm Coriander (*dhaniya*)
   powder
Salt to taste
2 cups / 500 ml / 16 fl oz Water
½ tsp / 1 gm *Garam masala*

Method

For the koftas, mix together all the ingredients. Divide this mixture into 16 even-sized balls.

Heat the oil in a wok (*kadhai*); deep-fry the koftas, a few at a time, until golden brown. Remove with a slotted spoon and drain the excess oil on absorbent kitchen towels. Keep aside.

For the gravy, boil the spinach and when cool, blend to a purée.

Heat the oil in a wok; add the garlic and spinach purée; cook for about 2-3 minutes. Stir in the tomato purée and mix well.

Add the red chilli powder, turmeric powder, coriander powder, and salt. Cook for 4-5 minutes. Pour in the water and bring the mixture to the boil. Stir in the koftas, reduce heat and let the mixture simmer for 5-7 minutes. Stir in the *garam masala* and cook till the curry has reduced to half. Remove from heat.

Carefully remove the koftas with a spoon and place them on a serving dish. Pour the curry on top and serve hot with any Indian bread.

Rogani Mushrooms

Mushrooms cooked in a rich onion and tomato curry

Ingredients

600 gm / 22 oz Mushrooms (*guchhi*),
  without stems, boiled
½ cup / 100 ml / 3½ fl oz Vegetable
  oil
4 Bay leaves (*tej patta*)
1 tsp / 2 gm Mace (*javitri*)
4 Cloves (*laung*)
4 Green cardamoms (*choti elaichi*)
4 Black cardamoms (*badi elaichi*)
2 Cinnamon (*dalchini*), 1″ sticks
4 tsp / 24 gm Ginger-garlic (*adrak-lasan*) paste
1½ cups / 300 gm / 11 oz Tomato
  purée, fresh
Salt to taste
2 tsp / 4 gm Red chilli powder
1 tsp / 2 gm Turmeric (*haldi*) powder
2 tsp / 3 gm Coriander (*dhaniya*)
  powder
150 gm / 5 oz Brown onion paste
  (see p. 7)
¼ cup / 50 gm / 1¾ oz Yoghurt
  (*dahi*), whisked
½ cup / 125 ml / 4 fl oz Water
a pinch *Garam masala*
1 tbsp / 4 gm Green coriander (*hara
  dhaniya*), chopped
1 tsp Ginger, julienned
1 tsp Green chillies, julienned

Method

Heat the oil in a pot; add bay leaves, mace, cloves, green cardamoms, black cardamoms, and cinnamon sticks; sauté till they crackle. Stir in ginger-garlic paste dissolved in a little water and stir-fry till the water dries out.

Add tomato purée, salt, red chilli powder, turmeric powder, and coriander powder; sauté for 2-3 minutes or till the oil separates.

Add the brown onion paste and yoghurt; stir-fry for 2-3 minutes. Add the mushrooms along with water and cook on low heat until the curry thickens and the mushrooms are cooked. Remove from heat and transfer to a serving dish.

Serve hot, garnished with *garam masala*, green coriander, julienned ginger and green chillies.

Baghar-e-Baingan

Serves: 4
Preparation Time: 15 min
Cooking Time: 30 min

Aubergines tempered with fenugreek and garlic

Ingredients

500 gm / 1.1 lb Aubergines (*baingan*),
   medium-sized
8 tbsp / 48 gm / 1¾ oz Tamarind (*imli*)
1 cup / 120 gm / 4 oz Onions, chopped
2 tbsp / 36 gm / 1¼ oz Ginger (*adrak*) paste
2 tbsp / 36 gm / 1¼ oz Garlic (*lasan*) paste
3 tsp / 9 gm Sesame (*til*) seeds
3 tsp / 6 gm Coconut (*nariyal*), desiccated
3 tsp / 6 gm Red chilli powder
3 tsp / 4½ gm Coriander (*dhaniya*) powder
1 cup / 200 ml / 7 fl oz Vegetable oil
3 Curry leaves (*kadhi patta*)
2 tsp / 3 gm Cumin (*jeera*) powder
¼ tsp Fenugreek seeds (*methi dana*)
2 tbsp / 24 gm Garlic cloves, chopped
1 tsp / 2 gm Turmeric (*haldi*) powder

Method

Soak the tamarind in warm water and squeeze out the pulp. Quarter the aubergines without disjoining them from the stem.

Grind the onions and ginger-garlic paste together.

Roast the sesame seeds, coconut, red chilli powder, and coriander powder. Remove from heat. Add 1 tbsp water and grind to a fine paste.

Heat the oil in a pan; add curry leaves, cumin powder, fenugreek seeds, and garlic cloves; sauté. Add the ground spices, aubergines, tamarind pulp, turmeric powder, salt, and ½ cup water; cook on low heat till the aubergines become tender.

Serve hot with steamed rice.

Bharwan Shimla Mirch

Serves: 4-5
Preparation Time: 20 min
Cooking Time: 20 min

Stuffed capsicum

Ingredients

6 Capsicum (*Shimla mirch*), large
1 tbsp / 15 ml Butter / Vegetable oil
120 gm / 4 oz Spring onions, chopped
1 tbsp / 4 gm Green coriander (*hara
   dhaniya*), chopped
250 gm / 9 oz Cottage cheese (*paneer*),
   grated
Salt to taste
1 tbsp *Chaat masala*
4 Green chillies, chopped
2 tsp / 3 gm Cumin (*jeera*) powder

Method

Slice each capsicum from the top. Scoop out the seeds and keep the capsicum cups and slices aside.

Heat the butter / oil in a pan; stir-fry the spring onions. Add the remaining ingredients. Cook further for 4-5 minutes. Remove from heat.

Fill the cottage cheese mixture into the capsicum cups and cover each with the capsicum slice. Secure with toothpicks.

Preheat oven to 150°C / 300°F. Place the stuffed capsicum on a baking tray or skewer carefully and grill on charcoal for 8-10 minutes or till the skin develops golden brown spots. Remove the toothpicks and serve hot.

Dum ka Paneer

Slow oven cottage cheese

Ingredients

500 gm / 1.1 lb Cottage cheese
  (*paneer*) cubed
4 tbsp / 60 ml / 2 fl oz Vegetable oil
½ tsp Garlic (*lasan*) cloves, fried
1 tbsp / 25 gm Onions, fried
1 tbsp / 15 gm Onion seed (*kalonji*)
  paste
1 tbsp / 10 gm Cashew nut (*kaju*)
  paste
1¼ cups / 250 gm / 9 oz Yoghurt
  (*dahi*)
½ gm Saffron (*kesar*)
5 drops Vetivier (*kewda*) essence
1 tbsp Yellow chilli powder
4 tsp / 4½ gm Coriander (*dhaniya*)
  powder
Salt to taste
5 Green chillies, slit

Method

Mix the oil, garlic, onions, onion seed paste, cashew nut paste, yoghurt, saffron, vetivier, yellow chilli powder, coriander powder, and salt together.

Marinate the cottage cheese in this mixture for 30 minutes.

Transfer the cottage cheese with the excess marinade in an ovenproof dish. Seal the dish with dough and cook in a preheated oven (180°C / 350°F) for 20 minutes.

Remove from oven, garnish with green chillies and serve with *naan* or steamed rice

Khade Masoor ke Dal

Lentil flavoured with curry leaves

Ingredients

1 cup / 100 gm / 3½ oz Lentil
  (*masoor dal*), picked, washed
½ cup / 100 gm / 3½ oz Ghee /
  Vegetable oil
1 cup / 120 gm / 4 oz Onions, finely
  chopped
4 / 12 gm Green chillies, chopped
1 tsp / 6 gm Garlic (*lasan*) paste
1 tsp / 6 gm Ginger (*adrak*) paste
1 tsp / 2 gm Red chilli powder
1 tsp / 2 gm Turmeric (*haldi*) powder
12 Curry leaves (*kadhi patta*)
Salt to taste
1 Juice of lemon (*nimbu*)

Method

Heat the ghee / oil in a pan; add onions, green chillies, garlic and ginger pastes, red chilli powder, turmeric powder, and curry leaves. Fry for 3 minutes.

Add the lentil and salt. Fry for 4 minutes. Pour in 1 cup of hot water. Bring to the boil, cover, and simmer until tender and the ghee / oil surfaces. Add the lemon juice and stir.

Gobhi Mussallam

Baked spicy cauliflower

Ingredients

180 gm / 6 oz Cauliflower (*phool gobhi*), cut into florets
a pinch Turmeric (*haldi*) powder
Salt to taste
4 Bay leaves (*tej patta*)
Water as required
2 tbsp / 30 ml / 1 fl oz Vegetable oil
4 Cloves (*laung*)
4 Green cardamoms (*choti elaichi*)
2 tsp / 12 gm Ginger-garlic (*adrak-lasan*) paste
3 tbsp / 60 gm / 2 oz Butter
a pinch *Garam masala*
a pinch Red chilli powder
a pinch White pepper (*safed mirch*) powder
3 tbsp / 30 gm / 1 oz Cashew nut (*kaju*) paste
2 tbsp / 60 gm / 2 oz Yoghurt (*dahi*)
3 tbsp / 45 ml / 1½ fl oz Tomato purée, fresh
2 tbsp / 50 gm / 1¾ oz Brown onion paste (see p. 7)
¼ cup / 50 ml / 1¾ fl oz Cream

Method

Boil the water in a pan; add turmeric powder, salt, and bay leaves. Gradually, add the cauliflower and cook covered on medium heat till ¾th done.

Remove from heat and drain the water. Transfer the cauliflower to an ovenproof dish.

Heat the oil in a pan; add cloves and green cardamoms. Sauté till they crackle. Stir in the ginger-garlic paste dissolved in 2 tbsp water. When the water dries out, add the butter and the spices.

Mix the cashew nut paste and yoghurt in ½ cup water and add to the pan. Cook on low heat till it comes to the boil. Stir in the tomato purée and the brown onion paste. Cook covered for about 5 minutes and stir in the cream.

Remove from heat and pour over the cauliflower florets.

Bake in a moderately hot oven for about 5-10 minutes and serve hot.

Kamal Kakri Lajawab

Serves: 4
Preparation Time: 20 min
Cooking Time: 30 min

Lotus stems in an exotic curry

Ingredients

800 gm / 28 oz Lotus stems (*kamal kakri*), peeled, cut into 1½″ pieces discarding the ends, washed
1¼ cups / 250 ml / 8 fl oz Mustard (*sarson*) oil
1 cup / 250 ml / 8 fl oz Water
2 Cloves (*laung*)
2 Green cardamoms (*choti elaichi*)
2 tbsp / 6 gm Fennel (*moti saunf*) powder
1 tsp / 4 gm Salt
1 tsp / 1½ gm Cumin (*jeera*) powder
½ tsp / 1 gm Cinnamon (*dalchini*) powder
1 tsp / 2 gm Black cardamom (*badi elaichi*) powder
1½ kg / 3.3 lb Yoghurt (*dahi*), whisked

Method

Heat the mustard oil in a wok (*kadhai*); deep-fry the lotus stems till half cooked. Remove with a slotted spoon and drain the excess oil on absorbent kitchen towels. Keep aside.

In the same wok, add the fried lotus stems and water, bring to the boil. Add all the spices and mix in the yoghurt. Cook till the curry thickens and the lotus stems are tender, stirring regularly.

Serve hot.

Khatte Aloo

Tangy potatoes

Ingredients

600 gm / 22 oz Potatoes
½ cup / 100 ml / 3½ fl oz Vegetable oil

4 tsp / 24 gm Onion, chopped
2 tsp / 4 gm Cumin (*jeera*) seeds
½ tsp / 1 gm Turmeric (*haldi*) powder
1 tsp / 2 gm Red chilli powder
2 tsp / 3 gm Cumin powder
2 tbsp / 20 gm Cashew nut (*kaju*) paste
  (optional)
1 tsp / 2 gm Cloves (*laung*) powder
a pinch Cinnamon (*dalchini*) powder
Salt to paste
2 cups / 400 gm / 14 oz Yoghurt (*dahi*)

Method

Peel the potatoes and soak them in water.

Heat 1 tbsp oil in a pan; sauté the onion till brown.

Heat the remaining oil in a wok (*kadhai*); sauté the cumin seeds till they crackle. Add turmeric powder, red chilli powder, and cumin powder with ½ cup water.

Mix in the remaining ingredients and cook for 5 minutes. Add the peeled potatoes and seal the pan with dough. Cook on low heat (*dum*) for 30-35 minutes.

Remove from heat, transfer into a serving dish and serve hot.

Bharwan Aloo

Serves: 4
Preparation Time: 20 min
Cooking Time: 15 min

Potato baskets

Ingredients

8 Potatoes, large, boiled, peeled

For the filling
100 gm / 3½ oz Chickpeas (*kabuli chana*), boiled
1 tbsp / 4 gm *Chaat masala*
1 tbsp / 24 gm Ginger (*adrak*), finely chopped
2 Green chillies, finely chopped
1 tbsp / 4 gm Green coriander (*hara dhaniya*), finely chopped
2 tbsp / 30 ml / 1 fl oz Lemon (*nimbu*) juice
Salt to taste

Method

Cut the potatoes in half and carefully scoop out the centres leaving a ½-shell behind.

For the filling, mix the chickpeas, *chaat masala*, ginger, green chillies, green coriander, lemon juice, and salt together. Press the filling into the potato shells.

Serve on a flat dish, hot or cold.

Kadhai Mushroom

Morel mushrooms in a hot tomato sauce

Ingredients

800 gm / 28 oz Morel mushrooms (*guchhi*), washed, halved
4 tbsp / 60 ml / 2 fl oz Vegetable oil
10 Dry red chillies (*sookhi lal mirch*)
½ cup / 60 gm / 2 oz Onions, chopped
6 tsp / 36 gm / 1¼ oz Ginger (*adrak*) paste
6 tsp / 36 gm / 1¼ oz Garlic (*lasan*) paste
3 tsp / 6 gm Garam masala
1 tsp / ½ gm Dry fenugreek leaves (*kasoori methi*), powdered
350 gm / 12 oz Tomatoes, deseeded, skinned
Salt to taste
2 tsp / 4 gm Coriander (*dhaniya*) seeds, roasted, crushed
½ tsp / 2 gm Black peppercorns (*sabut kali mirch*)
6-8 Green chillies, slit
3 tsp / 12 gm Green coriander (*hara dhaniya*), chopped

Method

Heat the oil in a pan; add dry red chillies and onions. Sauté and then add ginger-garlic pastes. Cook on medium heat. Add *garam masala*, fenugreek powder, and tomatoes, continue to cook on medium heat until the oil separates.

Add the morel mushrooms carefully and toss on high heat until the mushrooms are well coated. Cook for 5-6 minutes, stirring occasionally.

Add the salt, coriander seeds, black peppercorns, green chillies, and green coriander; mix well. Serve hot.

Guchhi Bhutte ki Subzi

Serves: 4
Preparation Time: 10 min
Cooking Time: 35 min

Morel mushrooms and corn bonanza

Ingredients

500 gm / 1.1 lb Morel mushrooms
  (*guchhi*)
250 gm / 9 oz Sweet corn (*bhutta*)
5 tbsp / 75 ml / 2½ fl oz Vegetable oil
4 Green cardamoms (*choti elaichi*)
3 Cloves (*laung*)
a pinch Mace (*javitri*) powder
2 tsp / 12 gm Ginger (*adrak*) paste
2 tsp / 12 gm Garlic (*lasan*) paste
½ cup / 150 gm / 5 oz Onion paste
6 tbsp / 60 gm / 2 oz Cashew nut (*kaju*)
  paste
1¼ cups / 250 gm / 9 oz Yoghurt (*dahi*)
4 Green chillies, slit
Salt to taste
½ cup / 100 ml / 3½ fl oz Cream
3 tbsp / 12 gm Green coriander (*hara
  dhaniya*), chopped

Method

Heat the oil in a heavy-bottomed pan; add green cardamoms, cloves, and mace powder. When they start spluttering, add the ginger and garlic pastes. Mix well. Add the onion and cashew nut pastes. Cook for 5-6 minutes more.

Add the yoghurt, green chillies, salt, morel mushrooms, and corn; simmer for 20 minutes.

Mix in the cream and green coriander. Remove and serve with puri (see p. 124).

Kurkuri Bhindi

Crunchy okra

Ingredients

500 gm / 1.1 lb Okra (*bhindi*), cut
   lengthwise into 4 slices
Salt to taste
1 tsp / 2 gm Red chilli powder
1 tsp / 2 gm *Garam masala*
½ tsp / 1 gm Mango powder
   (*amchur*)
½ tsp / 1 gm *Chaat masala*
3 tbsp / 30 gm / 1 oz Gram flour
   (*besan*)
Vegetable oil for frying
1½ tsp / 9 gm Ginger (*adrak*),
   julienned
2 Green chillies, sliced (optional)

Method

Spread the okra on a flat dish and sprinkle salt, red chilli powder, *garam masala*, mango powder, and *chaat masala*. Mix gently.

Now, add gram flour and mix gently to coat evenly, preferably without adding any water. Divide the okra into 2 portions.

Heat the oil in a pan to smoking point. Fry 1 portion of the okra mixture, separating each lightly with a fork. Do not allow the slices to stick to each other. Remove with a slotted spoon when evenly crisp and brown. Similarly, fry the other portion.

Serve hot garnished with ginger and green chillies.

Accompaniments

Broccoli Gajar Pulao

Broccoli and carrot pulao

Ingredients

2 cups / 400 gm / 14 oz Rice,
  Basmati, soaked for 10 minutes
150 gm / 5 oz Broccoli, cut into
  small florets
100 gm / 3½ oz Carrots (*gajar*),
  diced, parboiled
2 tbsp / 30 ml / 1 fl oz Vegetable oil
1½ tsp / 3 gm Cumin (*jeera*) seeds
1 Bay leaf (*tej patta*)
3 Cloves (*laung*)
1 tsp / 2 gm Black peppercorns
  (*sabut kali mirch*)
Salt to taste
6 cups / 1½ lt / 48 fl oz Water

Method

Heat the oil in a heavy-bottomed pan; add cumin seeds, bay leaf, cloves, and black peppercorns. When they start crackling, add carrots, broccoli, and salt. Stir-fry for 3-4 minutes.

Remove and discard the whole spices and keep the vegetables aside.

In a separate pot, bring the water to the boil, add rice and cook until done. Drain the excess water.

Gently mix the cooked vegetables with the rice and serve hot with any curry dish.

Nimbu Bhat

Lemon rice

Ingredients

½ cup / 100 gm / 3½ oz Rice,
  Basmati
2 cups / 500 / 16 fl oz Water
1 tsp / 4 gm Salt
3 tbsp / 45 ml / 1¼ fl oz Vegetable oil
  / Ghee
½ cup / 60 gm / 2 oz Cashew nuts
  (*kaju*), chopped
½ tbsp Black gram, split (*dhuli urad
  dal*)
1 tsp / 3 gm Mustard seeds (*rai*)
2-3 Dry red chillies (*sookhi lal mirch*)
½ tsp / 1 gm Turmeric (*haldi*)
  powder
6 tbsp / 90 ml / 3 fl oz Lemon
  (*nimbu*) juice
3 tbsp / 12 gm Green coriander (*hara
  dhaniya*), coarsely chopped
5 tsp / 25 gm Coconut (*nariyal*),
  fresh, shredded

Method

Wash and soak the rice in water for 10 minutes. Drain and keep aside.

Boil water in a heavy-bottomed pan. Stir in rice, salt, and ½ tbsp oil. Cover tightly, reduce heat and simmer without stirring until the rice is fluffy and tender and the water is fully absorbed. Keep aside.

Heat the remaining oil in a small pan. Stir-fry the cashew nuts until golden brown. Spoon cashew nuts over the cooked rice and replace cover.

Raise the heat slightly. Sauté the split black gram and mustard seeds. Add dry red chillies and remove from heat.

Gently fold in the sautéed mixture along with turmeric powder, lemon juice, green coriander, and coconut.

Serve hot, with plain yoghurt.

Guchhi Pulao

Morel mushrooms with rice

Ingredients

1 cup / 200 gm / 7 oz Rice, cleaned,
    drained
50 gm / 1¾ oz Morel mushrooms
    (*guchhi*), soaked in warm water for ½
    hour, drained
1 cup / 200 gm / 7 oz Ghee
2 Cinnamon (*dalchini*), 1″ sticks
6 Cloves (*laung*)
3 Green cardamoms (*choti elaichi*)
1 tsp / 2 gm Black cumin (*shah jeera*)
    seeds
½ cup / 60 gm / 2 oz Onions, chopped
Salt to taste
2 cups / 500 ml / 16 fl oz Water

Method

Heat the ghee in a wok (*kadhai*); add cinnamon sticks, cloves, green cardamoms, black cumin seeds, and onions. Sauté till the onions turn light brown. Add the rice and salt. Fry for 3 minutes.

Add the mushrooms and water. When the rice mixture comes to the boil, reduce heat and cook covered till the rice is done and the water is absorbed.

Serve hot.

Biryani-e-Dum Pukht

Serves: 4-5
Preparation Time: 30 min
Cooking Time: 45 min

Flavoured rice cooked with lamb   Picture on facing page

Ingredients

1 kg / 2.2 lb Lamb

For the rice
2½ cups / 500 gm / 1.1 lb Rice, Basmati
6 Green cardamoms (*choti elaichi*)
10 Cloves (*laung*)
2 Cinnamon (*dalchini*), 1″ sticks
1 tsp / 2 gm Cumin (*jeera*) seeds
½ Nutmeg (*jaiphal*)
3-4 blades Mace (*javitri*)
8 cups / 2 lt / 64 fl oz Water
5 Bay leaves (*tej patta*)
a few strands Saffron (*kesar*), mixed with 1 tbsp water or milk

50 gm / 1¾ oz Garlic (*lasan*)
1 Ginger (*adrak*), 1″ piece
1¼ cups / 250 gm / 9 oz Ghee
2 tbsp / 25 gm Onions, sliced
1 tsp / 2 gm Cloves, powdered
1 tsp / 3 gm Mace
1 tsp / 2 gm Cinnamon sticks, powdered
5 Green cardamoms, powdered
Salt to taste
¾ cup / 150 gm / 5 oz Yoghurt (*dahi*)
2 tsp / 4 gm Yellow chilli powder
a few strands Saffron
1 sprig Mint (*pudina*) leaves
1 tsp / 5 ml Vetiver (*kewda*) essence
2 Onions, medium-sized, sliced, browned
1 tsp / 2 gm Black cumin (*shah jeera*) seeds
1 Lemon (*nimbu*) juice
1¼ cups / 250 ml / 9 fl oz Cream

Method

For the rice, tie all the spices except bay leaves, in a muslin cloth. Immerse in water and bring to the boil. Add rice and bay leaves. Cook till the rice is half done; drain out the water and spread the rice on a tray.

Colour half the rice with the saffron mixture. Mix the white and the saffron-coloured rice together. Keep aside.

Grind ginger and garlic together and squeeze the extract.

Heat the ghee in a pan; brown the onions and keep aside to cool. Then grind and mix with the lamb. Add ginger-garlic extract.

Mix in the powdered cloves, mace, cinnamon, green cardamom, and salt.

Cook the lamb in a wok (*kadhai*) till brown. Add yoghurt and yellow chilli powder. Mix well.

Once the gravy thickens, add a little water. When the lamb is tender, remove the lamb pieces, and strain the gravy. Grind the saffron and blend into the cooked lamb.

Mix the strained gravy with the lamb.

Line the bottom of the pan with ghee, add one layer of rice, then a layer of lamb curry. Repeat till all the rice and curry are used up. The last layer should be of rice.

Sprinkle the mint leaves, vetiver essence, fried onions, and black cumin seeds on top of the rice. Add lemon juice and cream, close the lid tightly and seal with dough.

Keep the pan over a slow charcoal fire with a few live charcoals on the lid for about 45 minutes. This is the traditional way of making biryani. You can also keep it in the oven for 30 minutes. Serve hot.

Jhinga Biryani

Rice cooked in delicate spices and garnished with prawns

Ingredients

1¾ cups / 350 gm / 12 oz Rice,
  Basmati, washed
100 gm / 3½ oz Prawns, shelled,
  deveined
a pinch Turmeric (*haldi*) powder
1 Juice of lemon (*nimbu*)
1 tbsp / 15 ml Vegetable oil
1 Cinnamon (*dalchini*), 1˝ stick
4 Green cardamoms (*choti elaichi*)
2 Black cardamoms (*badi elaichi*)
4 Cloves (*laung*)
4 Bay leaves (*tej patta*)
2 tbsp / 50 gm / 1¾ oz Onion, sliced
2 tsp / 12 gm Ginger-garlic (*adrak-
  lasan*) paste
3 cups / 750 ml / 24 fl oz Water
2 tsp / 8 gm Salt
½ cup / 100 gm / 3½ oz Butter
3 tbsp / 45 ml / 1½ fl oz Milk

Method

Soak the rice for half an hour. Drain and keep aside.

Boil 2 cups water. Add salt, turmeric powder, and ½ lemon juice. Add prawns and cook till ¾th done. Remove, cut into small pieces and keep aside.

Heat the oil in a pot; crackle whole spices. Sauté onion till light brown. Add ginger-garlic paste dissolved in 1 tbsp water. Add the water and bring to the boil. Add salt, 90 gm/ 3 oz butter, remaining lemon juice, and rice; cook on medium heat, stirring occasionally till the water has reduced to the level of rice. Sprinkle milk, cover with a wet cloth and cook on low heat for 15 minutes. Transfer the rice onto a serving dish. Sauté the prawns in the remaining butter and sprinkle over the rice. Serve hot.

Plain Puri

Unleavened wholewheat fried, puffed bread

Ingredients

1¼ cups / 125 gm / 4 oz Wholewheat flour (*atta*)
Salt to taste
2 tsp / 10 ml Vegetable oil
½ cup / 125 ml / 4 fl oz Water
Vegetable oil for deep-frying

Method

Sift the wholewheat flour and salt together. Add oil and mix well.

Make a well in the flour mixture, add cold water and knead into a hard dough.

Divide the dough into 25 equal-sized balls and place them on a lightly floured surface. Cover with a kitchen cloth for 5-10 minutes.

Flatten each ball between the palms to make a disc, 4.5 cm in diameter. Roll out each of them to form a 10 cm disc.

Heat the oil in a wok (*kadhai*); deep-fry the discs until they puff up. Remove and drain on paper towels. Serve hot.

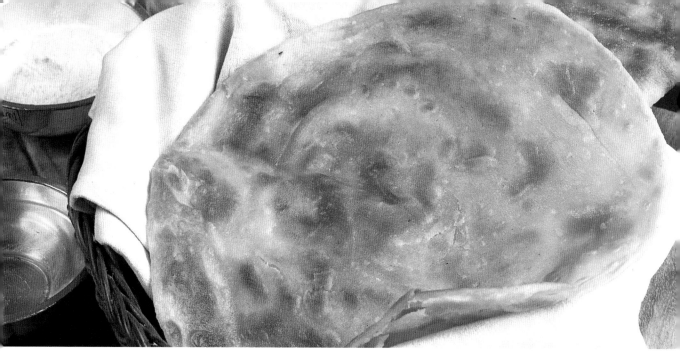

Lachha Paratha

Serves: 4-5
Preparation Time: 1½ hrs
Cooking Time: 30 min

Shallow-fried layered unleavened bread

Ingredients

4 cups / 400 gm / 14 oz Refined flour
  (*maida*)
Salt to taste
1¼ cups / 250 ml / 9 oz Milk
2 tsp / 4 gm Fennel (*moti saunf*),
  pounded
¾ cup / 150 gm / 5 oz Ghee
Ghee for shallow-frying
½ cup / 125 ml / 4 fl oz Water

Method

Sift flour and salt together. Make a well in the mixture and pour in the milk and water. Mix gradually and knead into a dough. Cover with a moist cloth and keep aside for 10 minutes.

Melt ½ cup ghee, add to the dough, kneading constantly to make it soft and smooth. Add fennel and knead again for 5 minutes.

Divide into 12 equal balls, dust lightly and roll into 6 discs. Apply 1 tsp ghee evenly over one side.

Make a radial cut and fold the disc into a narrow conical shape. Place flat side of the cone on the palm and twist palms together in a round movement to compress the dough into a thick flat round (*pedha*). Dust with flour, roll it out into an 8 disc. Refrigerate for an hour on butter paper.

Heat the griddle and shallow-fry the paratha on both sides on low heat till golden.

Serve hot with *raita* (see p.129).

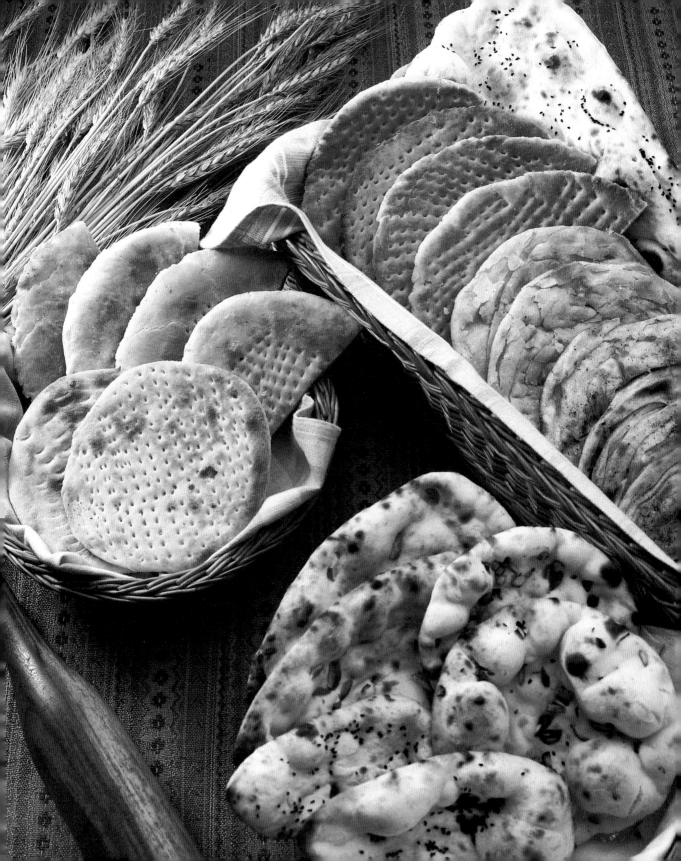

Naan

A light, levened bread

Ingredients

2 cups / 200 gm / 7 oz Refined flour
   (*maida*)
Salt to taste
¼ tsp Baking soda
1 tsp / 6 gm Baking powder

Whisk together
3 tbsp / 45 ml / 1½ fl oz Milk
2 tsp / 6 gm Sugar
5 tsp / 25 gm Yoghurt (*dahi*)

2 tbsp / 30 ml / 1 fl oz Vegetable oil
1 tsp / 1½ gm Onion seeds (*kalonji*)
1 tsp / 3 gm Melon (*magaz*) seeds
Ghee for greasing the baking tray
2 tbsp / 40 gm / 1¼ oz White butter

Method

Sieve the first 4 ingredients onto a kneading platter. Make a well in the centre; mix in 1 cup water and milk mixture and knead to make a dough. Cover with a moist cloth and keep aside for 10 minutes.

Add oil and knead again. Cover the dough and keep aside for 2 hours till it rises. Divide the dough into 6 balls. Flatten balls and sprinkle onion and melon seeds. Cover and keep aside for 5 minutes.

Roll and flatten each ball between your palms. Stretch the dough to one side to give an elongated shape (*naan*). Using oven gloves, stick the naan inside a hot tandoor for 3 minutes or place the naan on a greased tray and bake in an oven for 10 minutes at 180°C / 350°F. Apply butter (optional) and serve.

Tandoori Roti

Baked unleavened bread

Ingredients

2½ cups / 250 gm / 9 oz Wholewheat
   flour (*atta*)
1 tsp / 4 gm Salt
1 tbsp / 15 ml Vegetable oil
½ cup / 125 ml / 4 fl oz Water
Butter for greasing the baking tray

Method

Sift the flour and salt together. Mix in the oil and water; knead to make a soft dough. Cover with a moist cloth and keep aside for 30 minutes.

Divide the dough equally into 5 balls and dust with flour.

Heat the oven to 180°C / 350°F; flatten the balls and roll each out to an 8″ disc. Place the discs on a greased tray and bake for 3 minutes till pale brown in colour.

Serve hot.

Mixed Raita

Serves: 4-5
Preparation Time: 15 min
Cooking Time: 15 min

Mixed vegetables in yoghurt

Ingredients

2½ cups / 500 gm / 1.1 lb Yoghurt
(*dahi*)
1 tsp / 2 gm Cumin (*jeera*) seeds
1 tsp / 2 gm Coriander (*dhaniya*)
seeds
½ tsp / 1 gm Black peppercorns
(*sabut kali mirch*)
Salt to taste
½ Cucumber (*khira*), medium-sized,
chopped
2 Green chillies, finely chopped
1 tsp / 2 gm Mint (*pudina*) leaves,
finely chopped
3 tbsp / 36 gm / 1¼ oz Onions,
chopped
30 gm / 1 oz Tomatoes, chopped
a pinch Red chilli powder

Method

Heat a griddle (*tawa*) and broil the cumin seeds, coriander seeds, and black peppercorns till dark and aromatic. Pound and keep aside.

Whisk the yoghurt with salt. Add all the vegetables.

Pour into a glazed earthenware bowl. Sprinkle some red chilli powder and the pounded spices.

Serve chilled.

Variation: *60 gm / 2 oz squeezed pineapple chunks can also be added.*

Desserts

Chenna Payas

Serves: 4-5
Preparation Time: 20 min
Cooking Time: 45 min

Soft cottage cheese pellets in thickened milk

Ingredients

For the soft cottage cheese (*chenna*)
12½ cups / 2½ lt / 48 fl oz Milk
2 tbsp / 30 ml / 1 fl oz White vinegar
(*safed sirka*) or lemon (*nimbu*) juice

For the sugar syrup
2 cups / 300 gm / 11 oz Sugar
1 cup / 250 ml / 8 fl oz Water
5 tsp / 25 gm Refined flour (*maida*)

For the thickened milk (*rabri*)
3 tbsp / 60 gm / 2 oz Sugar
5 cups / 1 lt / 32 fl oz Milk
½ tsp / 1 gm Green cardamom (*choti elaichi*) powder
2 tsp / 2 gm Saffron (*kesar*)

2 tsp / 10 gm Almonds (*badam*), slivered
2 tsp / 10 gm Pistachios (*pista*), slivered
a few strands Saffron

Method

Boil the milk in a pan; add white vinegar or lemon juice to curdle. Reduce heat. Drain the whey and mash the curd cheese well. Keep aside.

For the sugar syrup, boil the water in a pot, add the sugar and stir continuously till the sugar dissolves completely.

Bring the syrup to the boil, lower heat, add refined flour and simmer. Allow to froth while the syrup is simmering.

Meanwhile, make 40 pellets from ¾th of the curd cheese. Gently slide these into the syrup. Continue to simmer until they swell to double their size. Remove the dumplings from the sugar syrup with a slotted spoon and keep aside.

Cook the remaining curd cheese in a wok (*kadhai*) on very low heat. Add sugar and stir continuously. Cook till the mixture begins to leave the sides. Remove from heat and keep aside to cool.

For the thickened milk, put the milk in a wok, bring to the boil and then simmer till it is reduced to $1/3$ rd. Add green cardamom powder and saffron; remove from heat and stir in the above mixture.

Return to heat and cook for about 10-12 minutes. Remove and keep aside to cool.

When cool, gently lower the dumplings into the mixture. Serve chilled, garnished with almonds, pistachios, and saffron.

Rosgolla

Cottage cheese dumplings in sugar syrup

Ingredients

7½ cups / 1½ lt / 48 fl oz Milk
3 tsp / 15 ml Lemon (*nimbu*) juice
2 tsp / 10 gm Semolina (*suji*)
2 cups / 500 ml / 16 fl oz Water
1½ cups / 225 gm / 8 oz Sugar
2 tsp / 10 ml Rose water (*gulab jal*)

Method

Bring the milk to the boil; add lemon juice to curdle the milk.

Pass the curdled milk through a muslin cloth. Tie the ends of the cloth and let it hang for 6 hours.

When all the whey is drained from the cottage cheese, add semolina and then knead well to make a smooth dough.

Divide the dough and shape into small lemon-sized, round balls.

Boil the water; add sugar and rose water. Cook till a thick syrup is obtained.

Carefully slide the balls into the syrup and cook until they become light and fluffy and start floating.

Kujja Kulfi

Serves: 4-5
Preparation Time: 2 hrs
Cooking Time: 30 min

Ice cream in earthenware moulds

Ingredients

5 cups / 1 lt / 32 fl oz Milk
3 tbsp / 60 gm / 2 oz Sugar
a few strands Saffron (*kesar*), soaked
  in 1 tbsp water
2-3 drops Yellow colour
a pinch Green cardamom (*choti
  elaichi*) powder
4 tsp / 20 gm Cashew nuts (*kaju*),
  chopped
1 tbsp / 15 gm Pistachios (*pista*),
  blanched, chopped

Method

Heat the milk in a wok (*kadhai*); cook on medium heat, stirring constantly till it is reduced to ¼th. Remove the wok from the heat and stir in the sugar till it dissolves completely.

Mix in saffron, yellow colour, green cardamom powder, cashew nuts, and pistachios.

Fill the mixture into earthenware moulds (*kujja*), cover with a lid and seal with any dough.

Place the moulds in a freezer for 1½ hours to allow the mixture to set.

Remove from the freezer, take off the lid and serve immediately.

Badam ka Halwa

Serves: 4-5
Preparation Time: 30 min
Cooking Time: 25 min

Almond delight

Picture on page 133 top

Ingredients

500 gm / 1.1 lb Almonds (*badam*),
  blanched, chopped
1 cup / 200 gm / 7 oz Ghee
1 cup / 200 ml / 7 fl oz Milk
3 cups / 450 gm / 1 lb Sugar
1 tsp / 2 gm Green cardamom (*choti
  elaichi*) powder
a few strands Saffron (*kesar*)
Silver leaf (*varq*), optional

Method

In a food processor, grind the almonds with a little milk to make a fine paste.

Heat the ghee in a heavy-bottomed pan. Add the almond paste and cook on medium heat until light golden.

Add milk and sugar, continue to cook for 10-15 minutes more till the moisture evaporates and the mixture becomes thick. Remove from heat. Add green cardamom powder and saffron.

To serve cold, spread on a greased tray, cut into small squares and decorate with silver leaf. To serve hot, ladle individual portions on to dessert plates and decorate with silver leaf.

Shahi Tukda Nawabi

Bread soaked in thickened flavoured milk

Ingredients

5 cups / 1 lt / 32 fl oz Milk
½ tsp / 1 gm Green cardamom (*choti elaichi*) powder
a few strands Saffron (*kesar*)
1½ cups / 225 gm / 8 oz Sugar
1 cup / 200 gm / 7 oz Ghee
8 Milk bread, slices

For the thickened milk (*rabri*)
10 cups / 2 lt / 64 fl oz Milk
½ cup / 75 gm / 2½ oz Sugar
½ tsp / 1 gm Green cardamom (*choti elaichi*) powder
a few strands Saffron (*kesar*)
2 tsp / 10 gm Almonds (*badam*), slivered
2 tsp / 10 gm Pistachios (*pista*), slivered

Method

Bring the milk to the boil in a heavy-bottomed pan. Add green cardamom powder and saffron. Remove from heat, add sugar. Keep aside.

Heat the ghee in a pan; fry the slices of bread lightly. Remove, drain the excess oil. Soak the fried bread in the milk mixture for 10 minutes.

For the thickened milk (*rabri*), heat the milk and cook till it is reduced to ¹/3 rd. Stir in the sugar, green cardamom powder, and saffron. Remove from heat and keep aside to cool.

Carefully lift the slices of bread from the milk and place on a serving platter. Pour the rabri on top and garnish with almonds and pistachios.

Serve chilled or at room temperature.

Gajar ka Halwa

Serves: 4-5
Preparation Time: 20 min
Cooking Time: 45 min

Shredded carrot pudding

Ingredients

1 kg / 2.2 lb Carrots (*gajar*), washed, peeled, shredded
2½ cups / 500 ml / 16 fl oz Milk
½ cup / 75 gm / 2½ oz Sugar
½ cup / 75 gm / 2½ oz Brown sugar
1 tsp / 2 gm Green cardamom (*choti elaichi*) powder
4 tbsp / 60 gm / 2 oz Ghee
2 tbsp / 30 gm / 1 oz Almonds (*badam*), slivered
2½ tbsp / 25 gm Raisins (*kishmish*)
2½ tbsp / 40 gm Walnuts (*akhrot*),
½ tsp / 1 gm Cloves (*laung*), ground
½ tsp / 1 gm Nutmeg (*jaiphal*), ground
½ tsp / 1 gm Cinnamon (*dalchini*), ground

Method

Boil the carrots and milk in a pan. Reduce heat to moderate and cook for 20-25 minutes, stirring continuously, till the mixture is nearly dry.

Add both the sugars and half of the green cardamom powder, stirring continuously for 10-12 minutes. Remove and keep aside.

Heat the ghee in a pan on moderate heat; fry the almonds until golden. Add the carrot mixture, raisins, chopped walnuts, and ground spices. Cook till the mixture begins to separate from the sides.

Serve hot garnished with the remaining green cardamom powder.

Imarti

Serves: 4-5
Preparation Time: 1 hr
Cooking Time: 45 min

Lentil roundels dipped in sugar syrup   Picture on facing page

Ingredients

1¼ cups / 250 gm / 9 oz Lentil (*masoor dal*), washed, soaked for 1 hour
1 tsp / 5 ml Yellow colour
5 tsp / 25 gm Refined flour (*maida*)
5 tsp / 25 gm Cornflour

For the sugar syrup
6 cups / 900 gm / 2 lb Sugar
6 cups / 1½ lt / 48 fl oz Water
a few strands Saffron (*kesar*)
1 tsp / 5 ml Vetivier (*kewda*) essence
3¾ cups / 750 gm / 26 oz Ghee

Method

Drain the lentil and blend to a coarse paste. Add yellow colour, flour, and cornflour. Keep aside.

For the sugar syrup, boil the water and sugar for about 20 minutes till the syrup reaches a thread-like consistency. Stir in the saffron and vetivier essence. Reduce the heat to low.

Heat the ghee in a shallow pan. Stuff the prepared paste into a cloth piping bag and pipe out the paste in circles, overlapping each other. Fry for 2-3 minutes on each side until golden yellow. Remove and immerse the roundels directly into the hot sugar syrup. Let them soak for 2 minutes.

Remove, drain the excess syrup and serve hot.

Zauq-e-Shahi

Fried dumplings served with thickened milk

Ingredients

½ cup / 100 gm / 3½ oz Wholemilk
  fudge (*khoya*), grated
4 tsp / 20 gm Soft cottage cheese
  (*chenna*, see p.7)
5 tsp / 25 gm Refined flour (*maida*),
  sifted

For the sugar syrup
½ cup / 125 ml / 4 fl oz Water
1 cup / 150 gm / 5 oz Sugar
Ghee for frying
a few strands Saffron (*kesar*)
4 tsp / 20 gm Pistachios (*pista*),
  chopped

Method

Knead the wholemilk fudge, soft cottage cheese, and flour into a
smooth dough with a little water. Divide the dough into 20 equal-
sized balls.

Make thin sugar syrup by boiling the water and sugar together.
Keep aside.

Heat the ghee in a wok (*kadhai*) on low heat. Slide the balls and
gently fry evenly on all sides. When the balls rise to the surface,
increase heat to moderate and cook till dark brown.

Remove, drain the excess oil and immerse in the sugar syrup. Let
them soak till cool.

Spread a layer of thickened milk (*rabri*) (see p.132) on a serving
dish and arrange the dumplings on top. Serve hot, garnished with
saffron and pistachios.

Kesar Sandesh

Saffron-cheese fudge   Picture on page 130

Ingredients

½ tsp Saffron (*kesar*)
1½ cups / 300 ml / 11 oz Full-cream milk
4 tbsp / 60 ml / 2 fl oz Lemon (*nimbu*) juice
½ cup / 75 gm / 2½ oz Sugar, powdered

Method

Roast the saffron in a dry pan and pound to a fine powder. Dissolve in 2 tbsp hot milk. Keep aside.

Heat the full-cream milk in a pan on high heat; bring to a frothing boil, stirring continuously. Reduce heat and add lemon juice to curdle the milk. If the milk does not curdle, then add 1 more tbsp of lemon juice. Remove from heat and keep aside to cool.

Pour the cheese-whey mixture into a moist cheesecloth. Pick up the cheesecloth by its corners, twist it loosely just to seal the cheese inside and rinse under the tap for a few minutes. Hang the cloth for 20-30 minutes to allow the excess water to drain.

Remove the cheese on a clean work surface and crumble till it becomes fluffy and even. Blend in the sugar and knead till smooth and grainless.

Transfer the cheese-sugar mixture to a heavy-bottomed pan. Cook for 10-15 minutes or until the mixture becomes a little thick and glossy.

Divide the mixture into two portions. Mix the dissolved saffron into one portion till it turns yellow. Divide the yellow cottage cheese mixture into 2 portions again.

Spread three alternate layers of yellow, white and yellow mixture on a buttered tray to form a 2″-thick cake. Keep aside to cool and then cut into 1½″-thick squares. Arrange on a platter and serve.

Lavang Latika

Bengali flour crispies

Ingredients

For the dough
1 cup / 100 gm / 3½ oz Refined flour (*maida*)
2 tbsp / 30 ml / 1 fl oz Vegetable oil
a few strands Saffron (*kesar*), soaked in 1 tbsp water
4 tbsp / 60 ml / 2 fl oz Water

For the filling
60 gm / 2 oz Wholemilk fudge (*khoya*), mashed
2 tbsp / 30 gm / 1 oz Almonds (*badam*), slivered
2 tbsp / 30 gm / 1 oz Pistachios (*pista*), slivered
½ tsp / 1 gm Cloves (*laung*), powdered
2 tbsp / 40 gm / 1½ oz Sugar, powdered

For the sugar syrup
3 cups / 450 gm / 1 lb Sugar
3 cups / 750 ml / 24 fl oz Water

12 Cloves
Vegetable oil for frying

Method

Sift the flour and make a well in the centre.

Add the oil and saffron, mix well. Add water gradually, and knead to make a hard dough. Cover the dough with a moist cloth and keep aside for 15 minutes.

For the filling, mix the wholemilk fudge, almonds, pistachios, clove powder, and sugar together. Divide the filling into 12 equal portions.

For the sugar syrup, boil the water with sugar till the sugar dissolves completely. Then simmer for 2-3 minutes.

Divide the dough into 12 equal portions and shape each portion into balls. Roll out each ball into 6″-diameter pancakes.

Place one portion of the filling in the centre of each pancake and brush the edges with water. Fold the pancakes from one side to the centre and press firmly to seal in the filling. Repeat from the other side, to give a 2″-wide strip.

Keeping the folded side out, bring the two ends together to make a ring with the strip. Brush the edges with water and press them firmly down to the centre to form squares. Secure each square with a clove.

Heat the oil in a wok (*kadhai*); shallow-fry the squares on low heat till crisp and golden brown. Remove with a slotted spoon and drain the excess oil on absorbent kitchen towels.

Submerge these crispies in hot sugar syrup completely, turning gently. If required, soak for 2-3 minutes. Remove and drain the excess syrup.

Arrange neatly on a serving dish and serve.